Middle Schoolers, Meet Media Literacy

Media, Marketing, and Me Series

Current media literacy and economics books generally approach students as future participants. This book series provides fully developed lessons that address the reality today that children as young as elementary school–age are not only participating in, but are often targets of, the purveyors of persuasive information and goods. This series of lesson books is designed to help teachers train young people to understand the methods and rules of a system of which they are already a part so that young people can emerge better informed and have more awareness and control in their consumption choices. Whether the message comes from commercial peddlers ("You should buy this") or sociopolitical peddlers ("You should believe this"), students need the tools to recognize, deconstruct, and make truly self-aware responses to the ubiquitous "nudges" that will forever be a part of their consumer lives.

Containing explorations in media literacy, behavioral economics, and other social environmental sciences, these hands-on, student-centered activities challenge students to examine the manner and content of information that is disseminated in society, or, to borrow from *The Wizard of Oz*, to see the man behind the curtain even when told to ignore him. Other forthcoming books in series will be for high school teachers and elementary school teachers.

Middle Schoolers, Meet Media Literacy

How Teachers Can Bring Economics, Media, and Marketing to Life

Jim Wasserman
David W. Loveland

ROWMAN & LITTLEFIELD
Lanham • Boulder • New York • London

Published by Rowman & Littlefield
An imprint of The Rowman & Littlefield Publishing Group, Inc.
4501 Forbes Boulevard, Suite 200, Lanham, Maryland 20706
www.rowman.com

6 Tinworth Street, London SE11 5AL, United Kingdom

All figures created by authors unless otherwise noted.

British Library Cataloguing in Publication Information Available

Library of Congress Cataloging-in-Publication Data

Names: Wasserman, Jim, 1961– author. | Loveland, David W., 1973– author.
Title: Middle schoolers, meet media literacy : how teachers can bring economics, media, and marketing to life / Jim Wasserman, David W. Loveland.
Description: Lanham, Maryland : Rowman & Littlefield, [2019] | Series: Media, marketing, & me | Includes bibliographical references.
Identifiers: LCCN 2018043769 (print) | LCCN 2018051813 (ebook) | ISBN 9781475842197 (Electronic) | ISBN 9781475842173 (cloth : alk. paper) | ISBN 9781475842180 (pbk. : alk. paper)
Subjects: LCSH: Media literacy—Study and teaching (Middle school) | Economics—Study and teaching (Middle school) | Marketing—Study and teaching (Middle school)
Classification: LCC P96.M4 (ebook) | LCC P96.M4 W37 2019 (print) | DDC 302.23071/2—dc23
LC record available at https://lccn.loc.gov/2018043769

∞ ™ The paper used in this publication meets the minimum requirements of American National Standard for Information Sciences Permanence of Paper for Printed Library Materials, ANSI/NISO Z39.48-1992.

Printed in the United States of America

To our children. You inspire us to try to make the world a better place for those to come. It's Truly Ben a Journey!

Contents

Foreword

> The ultimate goal of media education is to make wise choices possible.
> —Center for Media Literacy, Statement of Philosophy of Education

Since economics is the study of choice and how we allocate limited but desirable resources, imagine how delighted we were at the Center for Media Literacy (CML) when we learned of Jim Wasserman and Dave Loveland's new book, *Middle Schoolers, Meet Media Literacy: How Teachers Can Bring Economics, Media, and Marketing to Life*. Finally, teachers everywhere have a comprehensive guide to making the connections between media literacy and economics, thanks to these two experienced high school teachers from Dallas, Texas.

Such connections aren't apparent to most people. Most media literacy practitioners and resources address social studies or language arts or civics, so that students learn to access, analyze, evaluate, create, and participate with media messages using qualitative skills. But since making choices and understanding how choices are represented to us and by us is the goal of media literacy, quantitative skills of analysis are just as relevant to media literacy as the qualitative skills—and yet the association is often missed to the point that math teachers or science teachers question why they should address media literacy at all.

This book synthesizes the concepts behind economics and behavioral economics to empower consumers to make better everyday choices in their everyday lives as consumers and producers of powerful media images, words, and sounds. Ultimately, media literacy provides a methodology for risk management in making choices—for assessing potential opportunities and negative outcomes, while employing critical analysis when both consuming and producing media messages.

Just as media literacy emphasizes the importance of understanding the economic structures behind media and information (to better understand the profit and power purposes behind media messages), Wasserman and Loveland explain the dynamics behind our economy, giving a succinct and effective description of economic structures behind command, traditional, and free-market or capitalist economies.

Then they explore how behaviors result from individual choices, whether these choices are rational or not. They explore the heuristics—or patterns of behavior—that behavioral economists have uncovered through years of research and how these heuristics may or may not produce true value but instead are driven by *perceptions* of value or utility.

Again, the relationship between media literacy and behavioral economics is powerful since media literacy offers rational heuristics or "ways of seeing" to counter the persuasive techniques that are embedded in media messages. Through frameworks that address the essence of media—authorship, purpose, creative techniques and formats, audience targeting and message reception, framing, and bias—media literacy encourages habits of mind that challenge what we see, say, and hear.

While media literacy practices do not provide answers to pressing issues, they do provide a process of inquiry through which to seek and explore answers and provide the basis for subsequent individual choices. In an economic sense, media literacy is a market-oriented or capitalistic approach to individual and social choices because media literacy empowers citizens to make informed, independent choices. This approach to media literacy illustrates why it is often seen as essential for democracy and a free-market economy and why it can be perceived as a threat to command or traditional economies, where questioning authority or the status quo is often discouraged.

Yet youth cannot be expected to operate successfully within such economic, cultural, and political structures if they don't understand how these structures operate and how they are represented to us and by us. The media world is a vast symbolic system that represents the economic, social, and political lives of all citizens. As youth mature and engage more with the world, encountering new information and facing new challenges are essential to their confidence and ability to navigate the global media culture that they are surrounded with and to making choices for themselves.

This media culture is enticing and, by design, compelling; it takes a deep understanding and practice over time to gain the know-how to think independently and act with agency. Media literacy, and an understanding of the economic purposes behind the global media world, provides the understanding that is now needed to operate in a world where content is no longer scarce—but plentiful—and information process skills are scarce indeed. Youth today have more choices than ever, and they must be prepared from an early age to make healthy and affirming choices for themselves, their families, and their communities.

One of CML's frameworks for making choices is called the Empowerment Spiral of Awareness, Analysis, Reflection, and Action. This framework is based on the work of Paulo Freire, and through a large longitudinal study, CML has evaluated its frameworks to provide evidence of media literacy's positive impact on student knowledge, attitudes, and behaviors. Students can learn about the impact of media and choices on themselves and their communities, and they are *eager* to embrace such active learning.

The study of choice—economics—and how choice is represented to us through global media—media literacy—are essential to the well-being of every citizen. How we decide, individually and collectively, is ultimately our destiny—and an understanding of economics and media literacy provides the foundation that all citizens need to make wise choices possible. We hope that every teacher embraces these new ways of teaching and learning that prepare students for life.

Tessa Jolls
President, Center for Media Literacy
Director, Consortium for Media Literacy
http://www.medialit.org

Acknowledgments

The authors would like to first, and foremost, thank their wives for their love, patience, and flexibility as we became sometimes "there, but not there" during the creation of this book. We clearly have better taste than y'all, however; look whom we each chose to be life partners! We'd also like to thank our students and fellow teachers for allowing us to work in "Speaking of media lit . . ." even when just talking about the weather. The crucible of education allowed us to bounce ideas off of so many smart people until those ideas evolve from vague, poorly-thought-through, or just plain wrong to, well, less so.

We'd also like to thank the editors and staff at Rowman & Littlefield, particularly Sarah Jubar. You steered us newbies to publication with an understanding hand and guiding tone. You are a teacher's teacher!

Finally, we'd like to thank our children. We know you are more "native" to the Brave New World of media saturation, but your feedback, willingness to show us how things work (or just turn on), and feigned attention to our explanations of your world (while you silently wondered when you could go back to it) helped us not only make our ideas more concrete, but reminded us that media literacy is a very real issue that affects very real people's lives, including those most dear to us.

Chapter One

Marketing and Media

The Twin Pillars of American Society

A GENERAL (AND GENTLE) INTRODUCTION

What do your students think of when they hear the word "economics"? Parent-like lectures on how to spend money wisely? Complex formulas and graphs of supply and demand? Boring professors? Economics is a lot of things, including those (maybe not the boring professors part!), but it is also much more.

A student not sure whether it's better to do homework or chill out with a video game? Will that hot new music group kids like be around in another year? What's the best thing for a group of friends to do together this weekend? Even why do folks want to hang around with some people but not others? That's all economics, too.

Economics is the study of choice. How do we make choices? What's the best way to make a decision? What factors, including media, influence our decisions?

Now, what do your students think of when they hear "media literacy" (or more commonly, "media lit")? Perhaps some will shout out "fake news" (though do they know what that means?), but more likely you will get blank stares and shrugs. Yet, these students live among a swirling ocean of economic and media influences that don't just shape their decisions but actually affect who they grow up to be as people (like fish affected by the water unseen to them or people by the air they breathe).

With this manual, you will not only be introduced to the basic economic and media lit concepts that drive this field of study; you will be able to assist students to learn how to answer questions like those above. Even more, students will not only get firsthand experience in making economic decisions, but will also develop skills of deconstructing "neutral" communication to see how such messaging is often presented with an intent to influence them without their conscious knowledge. These skills will lead them to make better choices as they continue to be lifelong consumers of products and information.

With each chapter, we will provide basic explanations of the economic concepts to help you lay the groundwork for your students. Following each section is a series of student-centered lessons that have students explore the world they are in now, rather than giving hypothetical, unrelatable future examples (such as buying a house to learn about interest rates). The key is for students to immerse themselves in the activity and then afterward step back and reflect on what they did, how they felt, what decisions they made, and, most of all, how what they just did will better inform them for future decision making.

WHAT IS ECONOMICS?

Economics is a **social science**. Biology, physics, and chemistry are natural sciences because they strive to unlock how the physical universe functions. Social sciences such as psychology, sociology, and economics, on the other hand, study human behavior. This can be very challenging, as humans are not always consistent, either between two humans or even one person two days in a row.

Consider two kids jumping off a high-dive at a swimming pool. They may do the exact same dive, but one did it because they love the feeling of flying through the air, while the other did it reluctantly, fearfully, and only because he was dared to do it and didn't want to look like a "chicken" in front of his friends. It would be a huge problem to try and take into account every different motive of every person's actions every day, but fortunately many social scientists have discovered that, erratic as humans are, in large enough numbers we tend to be erratic in the same patterns. In economics, this might be seen in people spending too much for a shirt because its style or color is suddenly cool, though the quality of the shirt is otherwise unchanged.

The study of such decision making, including both logical and illogical thinking, has come to be called **behavioral economics** and has been around since at least 1899 when Thorstein Veblen wrote *The Theory of the Leisure Class*, a book that looks into such things as why rich people who are otherwise good with money sometimes waste it by buying unnecessary and expensive things.

One might say behavioral economics (sometimes called **consumer economics** when it particularly focuses on the psychological factors that influence a person's decision to obtain, buy, or consume something) came into its own in 2017 when Richard Thaler, one of the pioneers of modern behavioral economics and a key identifier of how consumers are "nudged" toward decisions, won the Nobel prize in economics. We will be using that term, **nudging**, mostly in the same sense he does, meaning that an otherwise conscious, rational decision about economic matters[1] (which for us, includes consumption of information as well as goods) is affected by other forces, including conscious nonrational factors, such as looking for coolness (chapter 4) and subconscious messaging by producers or speakers (chapter 5).

For all social sciences, a common method of investigation is by survey. Surveys allow for social scientists to collect lots of raw data and then look for a common pattern or some suggestion of a general rule. Many of the lessons in here are built on simple surveys that students can conduct so that they can employ direct, student-centered investigation; move around in the "real world" as they consider the concepts; and, most of all, have fun. To the extent that these surveys are general and simplified for students, they are not the most airtight in variables but are, rather, designed more for students to get a taste of social science investigation. Still, students should observe some basic rules of conducting social science surveys:

- **Be safe!** Don't approach strangers unless adult-supervised and in a public place.
- **Be considerate.** If someone says they do not wish to participate, let them go. Try to take as little of their time as possible, and always thank them for their time at the end.
- **Be neutral.** You are not looking to prove your preconceived idea but to investigate the question by collecting data. Do not suggest an answer or response unless it is part of the survey. Repeat the question if necessary or say, "I'm sorry; I'm not allowed to say more."
- **Be thorough.** Write down all the data you are supposed to collect at that time. Don't leave out anything because you don't like the response. Don't say, "I'll do it later," as you may forget, and be sure to write your information down so that another person can understand your information even if you aren't there to explain it.
- **Be a detective.** Data gathered doesn't actually give you any conclusions. Be like a detective; the conclusions come from your mind as you put all the pieces together. Once you have your data, look for patterns, rearrange things, and then write up what you think the data shows.
- **Have fun.** Surveying people is an adventure; you never know where it will lead. If you have an open mind, there is no limit to what you can find out. If you are enthusiastic, you will find many more subjects will be so too, and you will get more data.

It would be a good to have your class write out these rules on a large piece of butcher paper or a poster and post it somewhere in the class to remind them of these rules throughout their investigations.

See **Lesson 1A—Socializing Science**

WHAT IS MEDIA LITERACY?

Literacy is generally thought of as the ability to read the printed word. As teachers know, however, fully understanding an author's message is much more than just decoding the literal language used. It's picking up nuance and implied messages and reading between the lines. A story may not explicitly say that two characters should be contrasted, but the author gives the reader every opportunity to do so (think of all the bad children in *Charlie and the Chocolate Factory* who are selfish and impetuous, compared to Charlie).

Media literacy also means that when an author tries to make the audience feel a certain way, whether in regard to a fictional character or in regard to a real-life issue, a reader can recognize the emotional nudge and then decide for herself whether to go along for the ride and enjoy the trip or be a bit removed so as to not be taken someplace emotionally they do not wish to go. Being truly literate in the reading sense, then, means less that someone has read all the great books, but rather that she is capable of reading them and getting all she can from them.

Reading seems to be an art, a skill, or at least a pastime we are losing.[2] More people today are gravitating toward visual media or blended visual/verbal media rather than predominantly word-based media such as books.[3] Even so, the skills that were so important in purely reading still apply, perhaps more so today as the messages come to media consumers with greater ease and encased in entertainment. The fast-moving and brightly colored video that someone watches on YouTube remains a message made by a particular person or group with a particular point of view that can affect the world perspective of those who consume it.

Added to this is the ubiquity of messaging: there is virtually no place one can go without being bombarded by not just **information** but **persuasion**. **Media literacy**, then, is the ability to critically evaluate, understand, and decode messages to discern the difference between information and persuasion, to see what is both explicitly and implicitly messaged, for the consumer of information ultimately to have more control of the diet of messaging he or she consumes.

See Lesson 1B—Information, Persuasion, and Balancing the Equation

HOW DO ECONOMICS, BEHAVIORAL ECONOMICS, AND MEDIA LITERACY INTERACT?

Let's say a typical student sees an ad for a pair of cool shoes. **Classical economics** would study how the student weighs the price and quality of the shoes against other available shoes in making his decision whether to buy or not. Behavioral economics would study the intangible, even illogical, factors that go into the student's decision. Maybe he saw cool kids or a sports hero wearing the shoes, or he thinks back nostalgically to when he once won a championship wearing the same brand, or the color and style of the shoes are the same as a favorite "lucky" pair he had years ago.

Marketing would then try to convince the student to seal the deal and buy the shoes, perhaps by showing an admired athlete or cool pop star wearing them or how a kid who wears them is suddenly seen as cool by his peers. With all three of these areas, note that the student/potential buyer is on the passive, studied side of the discipline.

With **media literacy**, the focus is turned around and our student-consumer takes the active role. How can the student recognize and break down all of the appeals being made to him to buy, and how can he decide which ones he wants to actually consider? How can the student be empowered with the tools necessary to be more in control of his own consumer decisions, whether it be with tangible products like shoes or intangible ideas like political or social opinions?

Note that media literacy does not tell the student he should or should not consider a particular factor or even not consume something; rather, the goal is to leave such a decision up to the student, but with him more fully aware of the nature and quality of the product or information proffered, the influences on him to consume, and the availability of alternative choices.

Behavioral economics and media lit go hand in glove, and to that end, to adequately educate students, one must cover the basic concepts of economics (chapter 2) and behavioral economics (chapter 3) to then see how media lit complements these disciplines and better empowers economic consumers (chapters 4 and 5) and consumers of media in general (chapter 8). To put it another way, the art of conversation starts with listening and understanding the message being conveyed before one learns how to respond.

OH WAIT! BEFORE WE BUCKLE UP AND START THE CAR, A NOTE ABOUT METHODOLOGY . . .

We will be suggesting throughout this book a number of recurring lesson formats. We should stress that all of these have been tested and found to work, but teachers should feel free to modify as they see fit (and let us know!).[4]

For example, a number of the lessons ask students to watch TV shows and movies. Students can't analyze media unless they get a taste of it! Of course, kids love the idea of being assigned to watch TV, but it is important to review that they are *not* just kicking back and watching, but actively viewing, recording, and analyzing what they see. It is left to the teacher's discretion in all cases whether the students can be assigned to do this on their own, with parental supervision, or as a group at school.

Another common lesson format is group discussion. There are so many ways this can be done, so we leave it to the teacher to decide, but four suggestions are proffered here:

1. ***Circle talk***: informal discussion in small groups and with few rules (to encourage open sharing), though many teachers use limits such as that no one may speak longer than one minute, everyone gets a turn, and there is an announced set time limit of discussion (five to ten minutes).
2. ***Socratic seminar***: more structured than a circle talk, the students are given open-ended questions (such as the lessons in this book provide) that they must come to class prepared to discuss. They should bring notes, which contain both their thoughts and specific examples (such as from media) that support their ideas. They should also have pre-written a paragraph on their view coming into the discussion. The teacher (or assigned student discussion leader) throws out one of the open-ended questions as a "jump ball." The students then discuss (perhaps observing the rules of circle talk). If a question gets talked out, the group moves on to another question. If there are a large number of students, one group can sit on the outside of the circle, taking notes, switching places with the inner circle every five minutes or new question. After the Socratic circle is completed, students then write a post-discussion reflection in which they indicate whether they have the same view, have modified their view, or completely changed, and why.
3. ***Fishbowl***: This is a structured discussion that is designed to have maximum participation and keep a two-sided conversation evolving. Four chairs are placed in the center, two for each view. Only the people in the middle may speak. Any comments from outside can cause point deduction (if scored). Once someone has spoken, she may

be tagged out by someone on the same side of the issue. The tagger then takes the seat and remains until he has said something and is tagged out. The person tagged can finish his thought, however, before leaving. All comments made by a person are owned by that side. If Johnny says, "Martians are behind all advertising" and Susie tags in for him, she is stuck with the statement (as the idea is for a continuously moving but generally cohesive discussion). If scoring, 1 point for a strong point made, 2 points for a strong rebuttal, and 3 points if a person specifically cites a source as support. Everyone must observe the rules of respect, including addressing issues, not the people making them (**ad hominem fallacy**).

4. ***Improv***: Finally, we also advocate using an **improv** format to add an element of fun. For those unfamiliar with it, students are divided into small groups (five is a good maximum)[5] in which they are given a general premise (buying something at a store) with certain specific elements (what they are buying) or interrupting events (a tornado or the store forgot to pay its gravity utility bill) happening and students must on the spot keep the action going and be creative in displaying and solving the problem. The new elements can be delivered either one or two minutes before performance (so that the group can plan) or put on an index card face down and turned over in the middle of the performance for immediate adaptation. Either way, the teacher should be equipped with multiple variables so no groups get the same ones (but get similar in kind). The main point is not to get it right but to keep the flow going and have fun. This format has been well-received at all levels of students; even naysayers usually get into it as the rest of the class has fun with it (but we'll explore peer pressure later!).

CHAPTER 1 ACCOMPANYING LESSONS

Lesson 1A—Socializing Science

Key Concepts

Economics as a social science, studying aggregated human behavior

Special Materials/Media

Computer to run spreadsheet program (optional if the teacher wishes to tie the lesson with spreadsheet usage)

Intro Questions/Thoughts for Students

- If you take a lot of individual things (like trees), can you make generalized statements about them when you look at large groups of them?

- Can you do the same thing with people? You are all individuals, with your own likes and dislikes, but do you think there are any patterns? What do you think those patterns would show?
- Can generalizations about groups of people be useful? When are they helpful and when are they not?

Activity

Introduce students to the scientific method in the following manner:

1. Ask students generally as a class if they think the members of the class are more similar or different. Then pose the two following specific questions: *What general statements can be said about the class as a whole? Which of such statements cover the most members of the class?* Explain to students that asking such **initial questions** is the first step to scientific inquiry and discovery, from Sir Francis Bacon to studying the edges of our universe today.
2. Students should now talk in small groups, each talking for roughly two minutes about himself or herself, including information about where they were born, favorite things, travels, or hobbies. Explain that the information they are generally gathering is part of the second step of experiments called **research**.
3. From this research, each student should now formulate a **hypothesis**, an educated guess or preliminary answer to the questions posed above.
4. Now it's time to **experiment**. In physical sciences, this usually means setting up a lab, but in social sciences, it often means conducting a survey to see responses (and sometimes altering the survey in different ways to see if the results vary). In this case, have students develop a survey that asks general questions, such as:

   - Your favorite and least favorite foods?
   - How many countries have you visited?
   - Where were you born?
   - Favorite music artist?

5. Have everyone in the class fill it out. If possible, have students from other classes/grades also fill out the survey.
6. Now comes the **analysis** and drawing **conclusions**. Have the students then tally results and try to formulate general statements, such as "We like superhero movies." They can also make pie charts to illustrate the general trends of "Who we are."

Follow-up Questions/Discussions

- Were you surprised by any "winners" in each category? How accurate were your initial hypotheses?
- Were any of your hypotheses way off? Is that bad? If someone had an incorrect hypothesis that proved to be unsupported by the data, what should he or she do?
- Were some trends by a lot or by a little? How is that important?
- Were the most popular responses a majority (over 50 percent) or a plurality (the most common but under 50 percent)?
- How could a person studying or doing a report on the class use this information? What about a **marketer** (someone trying to sell a product to the class)?
- What might be a problem of assuming all members of a group act or think in agreement with a majority of that group?
- A good researcher always takes a moment to not only analyze the data but look back and see if the methodology (way the experiment was run) might have an effect on the results or could be improved. Discuss some ways you could repeat the experiment but make it better:

    1. Ask more people (bigger sample size).
    2. Reword the question.
    3. Change the order of the questions.
    4. Change whether the survey is given as a group (where people might call out or look on other's responses) or done in private.

Social Questions for Students

- If one of your responses (such as your favorite movie) was the most common, how did that make you feel? What if your favorite was the least liked by others?
- Do we judge people by what they like? Should we? Is liking something unpopular the same as *being* unpopular? How can we distinguish between the two?
- Has someone ever assumed something about you because of the majority opinion of those you are friends with? How did that make you feel, especially if it wasn't true?

Lesson 1B—Information, Persuasion, and Balancing the Equation

Key Concepts

Distinguishing information versus persuasion

Special Materials/Media

Access to movie or restaurant reviews (such as Yelp) online, access to historical biographies, two colors of highlighters

Intro Questions/Thoughts for Students

- What is the difference between “information” and “persuasion”? When people communicate, do they mainly use one, the other, or both? When is each helpful?
- How can we tell the difference between information and persuasion?
- Can someone try to persuade by just giving selective information?

Activity

Have the class look up the definitions of *information* and *persuasion*. They should discuss the differences in groups and see if the class can arrive at an agreed definition and understand the difference between the two.

Students should then read restaurant or movie reviews, marking information statements (“The restaurant has three kinds of pasta”) in one color highlighter and persuasion statements (“The portions are too small”) in another.

As an additional exercise, students should choose (or be assigned) famous historical figures. One group of students must list facts (information) that make the historical figure look good or admirable (“George Washington was the first president”). The other group should list facts (information) that might make someone not admire the historical figure (“George Washington owned slaves”).

Follow-up Questions/Discussions

- Where do you find statements that are mainly informational? Where do you find statements that are mainly persuasive?
- Is it easy to distinguish information from persuasion? Can a statement like “The portions are huge” be *both* information and persuasion?
- What about selective information? Can knowing only part of the information be used as persuasion? Do people ever intentionally only give part of the information to persuade others?

Social Questions for Students

- Do you ever accidentally give your opinion when trying to be neutral? Have you ever only recounted “your side” in retelling a disagreement to a third person?
- Have you ever thought of someone as nice or rude but then found out more facts that changed your mind? Have you ever done anything that

appeared rude to someone, but there was an explanation or reason why? Perhaps write a letter to that person explaining the story behind what happened.

NOTES

1. Richard Thaler and Cass Sunstein, *Nudge: Improving Decisions about Health, Wealth and Happiness* (New York: Penguin Books, 2009), 8.
2. See Caleb Crain, "Why We Don't Read, Revisited," *The New Yorker*, June 14, 2018, https://www.newyorker.com/culture/cultural-comment/why-we-dont-read-revisited.
3. See Michelle Krasniak, "Visual Content and Social Media Marketing: New Research," Social Media Examiner, May 30, 2017, https://www.socialmediaexaminer.com/visual-content-and-social-media-marketing-new-research/; or Victoria Malabrigo, "Visual Content on Social Media: 2017 Trends and Research," WNET/New York Public Media Interactive Engagement Group, March 13, 2017, https://ieg.wnet.org/2017/03/visual-content-social-media-2017-trends-research/.
4. We are also cognizant that most of our lessons assume at least limited access to the Internet, and while, in this day and age, this should be unquestionably available for all students, it is unfortunately not so.
5. As improv is an intense but short-term cooperative challenge, a randomizer program of names, such as https://www.random.org/lists/ keeps groups new each time the exercises are done. On the other hand, teachers may find the exercise valuable to put particular students together to "nudge" them to appreciate and cooperate with each other. We won't tell!

Chapter Two

Introduction to Basic Neoclassical Economics (The Objective Study of Choice)

HOW TO INTRODUCE ECONOMICS TO THE CLASS

Economics is the study of choice and, in particular, how we allocate limited but desirable resources. There is no government agency devoted to preserving gravity because, though we find it essential, we aren't afraid of it running out anytime soon. On the other hand, when people became concerned we might use up or pollute clean air and water, Congress created the Environmental Protection Agency (EPA) in 1970 to help give advice and regulate the use of natural resources, so that we can make the best choices about how to use and preserve them. Economics doesn't really concern itself as much over how we use **free goods**, or things that are abundant and come at no cost (sunshine, gravity).

On the other hand, economics is really about studying our decisions in regard to **scarce economic goods and resources**. These are things of which there are few but that are in demand. Be sure to distinguish scarce goods from **rare goods**, which are things of which there are few but may or may not be wanted. Both diamonds and five-legged cats are rare, but since most people only want diamonds out of the two, the diamonds are also scarce.

How few of something does there have to be for something to be considered scarce? There is no set number; it's really just about there being fewer of the things desired than there are people who want them. In the 1990s, there were thousands of Beanie Babies produced, but because more people wanted them than there were the actual toys, they were scarce (and scary when adults got into shoving matches in toy stores over them!). So, when your students are deciding if they'll watch a TV show or play a computer game, they are engaging in an economic decision regarding using the scarcest resource of all: time (because you can never make more!).

See **Lesson 2A—Voice Your Choice**

See **Lesson 2B—Make Yourself Scarce!**

MONEY FOR NOTHIN' . . .

Even though odes and songs have been written for ages about having lots of money, it is important to remember that money is not the end goal for either producers or consumers (or, as will be often referred to here, sellers and buyers). Money itself is nothing more than a tool; it is a means to an end, with the end usually being for both sellers and buyers acquiring things that we perceive will make our lives better and more enjoyable, from food and shelter to vacations and computer games.

In a typical sale, money becomes important in two ways. First, money is used to make the product to be sold. As such, it is part of what economists call **factors of production**, which are the things used to make the product (or **good**) to be sold. Economists generally put all such factors into one of three groups:

1. **Land**—the raw materials used to make the good.
2. **Labor**—the persons who put in effort to make the good and bring it to sale.
3. **Capital**—the machines and tools used to make the good.

A simple example of the depth and complexity of these factors is your basic fast-food burger. Land factors include the meat, lettuce, grains, even down to the tomatoes that became ketchup. For labor, the obvious person one thinks of is the guy at the counter who sold it to you, but if you think of the long line behind him, it includes the cook, the person who delivered the food to the store, the warehouse people, continuing back to the farmer or rancher!

As for capital, there are all the machines and systems that went into bringing that meal to you, from the cash register back to the fryers to the trucks and tractors. It almost boggles the mind to think of yourself sitting in the middle of a circle composed of all the people and things that went into your one moment, so you better appreciate it and eat it all! Money falls into the capital factor, as it is a tool for the producer to acquire the land, labor, and machines that then make the burger.

Some economists add a fourth factor, **entrepreneurship** or **human capital**, to incorporate knowledge and particular skills someone such as a manager might bring in making a product. The inventor of the secret sauce recipe falls into this category, as does the efficiency expert who creates a kitchen to deliver food hot and fresh (or at least quickly).

The second place where money is important in a typical sale is when the consumer acquires the product from the producer. At that point, money is a **medium of exchange**, meaning it's an agreed-upon representation of a product's value. Before money, people traded goods for other goods (**barter system**), but this had severe limits.

For one, both parties had to want each other's goods for trade to happen. To help students understand, ask them to rate how much they like apples. One student may love apples and would give away ten of her pencils for one red delicious; another may not like them as much and so would only give away one or two pencils or none at all. Thus, we can't be sure as a group what an apple is worth, but with money, we can all understand what one dollar represents.

Money, whether metal coin or paper, also has at least two other advantages. First, it's easy to carry around (think of a rancher having to pull a steer out of his pocket!); second, it stores its value, meaning it doesn't turn bad very quickly like a bushel of bananas would. A wrinkled, dirty dollar is worth the same as a crisp new one.

***See* Lesson 2C—Money for Nothin'**

WHOSE CHOICE?

If economics is the study of rational choice making, then who is the central character? Who is the chooser? The short answer is that it depends on the economic system. There are three types of economic systems, roughly defined by who does most of the choosing.

In a **command economy**, the government and its agents and agencies decide things like what is produced, the prices, and who can buy the goods. Autocratic states, such as that of the former Soviet Union or dictatorships like North Korea, often have strong elements of this type of choice making, from designing the country's production plans for the next five to fifteen years down to assigning particular jobs to individuals, such as factory worker or gymnast.

In a **traditional economy**, one could say current participants are outvoted by all their ancestors, as choices are made based on tradition or custom. Various religious and cultural groups, such as Muslims, Jews, and Hindus, must abstain from choosing certain animals for food because of traditional religious dietary laws, just as many Christians abstain from meat on Fridays or other things during Lent.

Finally, in a **free-market** or **capitalist** society, choices are left up to individual sellers and buyers, including the ability to negotiate and bargain until there is an agreed-upon choice at an agreed-upon price. This freedom of choice makes the free-market system the most active in terms of marketing in order to affect consumer choices, and thus, as so many choices are left to the individual, it is the system wherein its participants need most to be informed consumers.

Which system does the United States have? While the United States was founded with a view toward a free market, and relative to many countries it adheres to that system, it's also important to note that almost no country, including the United States, functions by one system purely; most are an amalgam of all three. Visit a grocery store, and you'll see the food generally offered at the grocer's price (free market) but know that his selection of what kind of food offered, such as ten different kinds of chili in Texas, may be dictated by local custom (traditional), and all the food sold, and the store itself, must meet certain government-mandated health standards (command).

CHOOSING—THE TRADE-OFF

So, you are a student with a lot of homework (or a teacher with lots of grading), but you also want to see the latest episode of that TV show you love. It's a free-market decision, so the choice is up to you. How do you (and generally, all consumers) make the choice? First, let's recognize the scarce resource in this scenario: *time*. You don't have time to do both in one evening, so you'll need to *spend* your time on either the schoolwork or the TV show.

Most people have heard of the economic phrase *cost-benefit tradeoff*, which is generally thought of as comparing two products to decide which to buy. The student-chooser here might make a list and rate how much (1–10, 10 being high) each set of benefits means to him:

Benefits of choice A	Benefits of choice B
Schoolwork	TV show
• better chance for good grade • parents happy • helps me for next lesson	• entertainment • can talk about show with friends • helps me at next party
Score: **6**	**8**

As the TV show is an 8 but the schoolwork is a 6, it would seem the show wins. However, this is only half the job; it's only a benefit-benefit comparison. To do a real **cost-benefit analysis**, the student would do the following:

Benefits of choice A	Benefits of choice B
Schoolwork	TV show
• better chance for good grade • parents happy • helps me for next lesson	• entertainment • can talk about show with friends • helps me at next party
Score: **6**	**8**

Costs of choosing A	Costs of choosing B
Schoolwork	TV show
• miss out on show for one night • may have spoiler given away by friend • may give up another show to catch up	• parents disappointed • parents take away TV • behind other students • will have to give up another night to study
Score: **7**	**10**

(Note that the cost rating is still how much it affects him but this time *negatively*: how much it would *bother* him.)

Now, one more bit of movement. The costs (negatives) of choice A (schoolwork) really are benefits (positives) *for* choice B (TV show) and vice versa, so the *total* score would be:

Choosing A	Choosing B
Schoolwork	TV show
Benefits of A (6) + Costs of B (10)	Benefits of B (8) + Costs of A (7)
Score: **16**	**15**

Lo and behold, factoring in the potential negative consequences means the student should do the schoolwork. (Did you really expect different in an educational manual?) This may look complicated, but it is what we all do if we thoroughly consider options when making a choice. We may not list out pros and cons or assign formal numbers, but even an impressionistic, quick decision is made this way, even if at a gut level, and the beauty of this kind of analysis is that it works for just about every choice!

***See* Lesson 2D—Trade-offs Are On!**

INFLUENCES ON CHOICE

If we were to continue following the straight and narrow road of **neoclassical economics**, we would delve into the microeconomic world that revolves around supply and demand. However, our journey is less about moving further into "pure" economics than it is moving deeper into teaching students how we all choose, the rational and nonrational nudges on what is thought to be "our choice," and how we can better equip ourselves, through media literacy, to make informed choices as free as possible from invisible persuasion. Before we leave old-fashioned economics, however, we should delve into how more traditional economics does take note of many factors, mostly practical and rational, that can influence both the items that we might list in our cost-benefit analysis and how we assign value to them.

In the world of supply and demand, the idea of **consumer sovereignty** says that the consumers (demanders) not only make their decisions relatively independent from producers (suppliers), but that the collective body of consumers has more power than the collective body of producers when it comes to many, if not most, economic choices. It's easier for consumers to move on to another producer than a producer to just find new customers, so in essence the consumers get to call the tune by weighing cost-benefit factors as shown above.

The values in such a weighing are, in turn, determined by various factors within the consumer's rational mind, the most important being a product's usefulness to the potential buyer, or its **utility**. An extension of utility is **marginal utility**, or the satisfaction (benefit) we get from consuming (using) one additional product.

After school a girl stops by a convenience store, where she realizes she has two dollars. She is thirsty and hungry, but her thirst (on our always handy 1–10 scale) is an 8 and her hunger is a 6. Given she can buy either one drink or one snack, she will opt for the drink because it has a higher marginal utility. It will, relative to price, satisfy her more.

Let's say that, after she drinks, she finds two more dollars in her other pocket. She weighs her choices again, but now finds that whereas her hunger is still a 6, her thirst has dropped to a 5. This is because of the **law of diminishing return**, that for the same amount of resources put in (here, two dollars), one gets less benefit. It's a fancy way of saying things get old and explains why even the best party can get boring after a while or that one can only study so much. Back to our girl in the convenience store, because of the new comparative marginal utilities, she will switch her choice and purchase the snack, as it has the higher marginal utility now (6 compared to 5).

See Lesson 2E—No More, Please!

Even with all this subconscious, independent calculating, a consumer's decision is modified by outside factors. One factor is the availability of the products the consumer wants. The consumer may have done his cost-benefit analysis and is eager to buy, but the product is unavailable because the store has sold out (a *shortage*) or the price is not within his ability to pay. The fact that a rise in price usually means fewer consumers is actually given a fancy name, the **price effect**. Availability of a product is usually out of the control of the consumer and is more dependent on things like weather (for food), popularity, and how many were produced.

Another outside factor that affects consumers' rational choices is the availability of what are called **substitutes** and **complements**. Substitutes are things a consumer could buy *instead* of the intended product, such as ham instead of chicken at the deli. A group of kids may plan to go to the movies, but if they see a deal on getting tickets to a concert, the movie theater loses customers.

Complements, on the other hand, are products that *go with* the target product. Call out "peanut butter and . . ." to a class of American kids and they will almost unanimously say back "jelly" (unless they are Elvis fans, in which case you may hear "banana"). If the price of jelly goes down, you can bet the sales of peanut butter will go up as it tags along for the ride. Some producers try to get people to spend more by creating complements, whether it is creating new combinations of sandwiches or inventing "must-have" **accessories**, such as matching shoes and handbag.

See Lesson 2F—There's No Substitute for Your Complements

Neoclassical economics is an extensive social science that includes the study of consumers, for the most part, making independent, rational choices. Advertising's role in such a system is to convey information, such as price and quality, to help consumers make their rational decisions.

Look at just about any ad, however, and you'll find a lot more being said about a product than its price and quality. Some of the ads seem irrational, if not downright fantastical. Either all these advertisers are off the mark, or they know that there are other factors that consumers consider, maybe even ones consumers are not consciously aware of, making them vulnerable to advertisers sneaking extra factors into their cost-benefit analysis, like a cheap chef adding sugar to a dish to make it taste better. What are those nonrational appeals, and even more, what do consumers need to know about themselves to guard against ingesting unlisted ingredients? Welcome to behavioral economics and media literacy!

CHAPTER 2 ACCOMPANYING LESSONS

Lesson 2A—Voice Your Choice

Key Concepts

Economics as the study of choices/decision making, **scarcity**

Special Materials/Media

A log sheet, as below

Intro Questions/Thoughts for Students

- How often do you have to make choices in a day? Is there a pattern to your decision making?
- Is there a general rule you have in deciding between two choices?

Activity

Students keep a log for a day. Every time they are faced with a choice and decision, they should fill out a log (expand as necessary) as follows:

Choice A	Choice B	Why couldn't I have both?	Which did I choose?	Why?

Follow-up Questions/Discussions

- Do you see a pattern in the kinds of choices you have to make (such as food or activity) or a time when you make a lot of choices (lunch time)?
- Is there a recurring reason why you had to make a choice (lack of time, money)?
- Is there a pattern as to why you chose things? Does it fit the "general rule" you said before the activity (which became a **hypothesis**)?[1]
- Was this day "typical" of the kinds of choices you had to make? If not, why not?
- Can you write up your log as a lab report (hypothesis, data, conclusions, etc.)?

Social Questions for Students

- Are there circumstances or situations that make it harder for some people to make some choices than for others? Why is that?
- What would you do if you had a friend who was making bad, unhealthy, or even dangerous choices? Could keeping a log like this help them to see how they make bad choices?
- When would you rather not be given a choice but be told there is only one option to select?

Lesson 2B—Make Yourself Scarce!

Key Concepts

scarcity, creating **(false) scarcity**

Special Materials/Media

Access to Internet

Intro Questions/Thoughts for Students

- If you're selling something, would you rather your product be scarce or common? Why?
- How can you make something scarce?
- What is the scarcest thing that you can think of? Are there some things you can never get more of? What about time? Is time scarcer for some of you than others?

Activity

Have students look for things that are only good for "a limited time." It can be advertised sales, food with expiration dates, or homework assignments with a firm due date. For each, have the students discuss whether the time allotted is (1) necessary for a reason, (2) necessary but maybe artificially shortened (many food expiration dates are considered as such), or (3) arbitrary (there isn't a good reason to make it available for a limited time).

Follow-up Questions/Discussions

- Were there any general patterns as to what kinds of things were in each category?
- How can putting a time limit be helpful to either (or both) the seller/requester and the buyer/doer?
- Why would someone wanting you to buy/do something put a limited time on it? Did that make the product (or the opportunity to acquire/do the activity) seem scarcer and therefore more valuable and desirable?
- Besides limiting things by time, how else can a seller make what they have to offer special, and therefore scarce, so as to make you want it more?

Social Questions for Students

- Is it ethical for someone to make you feel a false sense of urgency to persuade you to do something? Does that violate a sense of trust and honesty or is that just good persuasion?

Lesson 2C—Money for Nothin'

Key Concepts

currency, money as a created system for exchange of value

Special Materials/Media

Quantities of different items found in a classroom or home, such as paper clips, pencils, pieces of paper or tape, sticky notes, etc.

Intro Questions/Thoughts for Students

- What is money?
- Why do we use it?
- How do we assign it value?

Activity

Your students' school (or learning center) is now its own country. It will take a while to get things up and running, but in the meantime, they will need some sort of money (**currency**) to buy and sell goods (food, pencils, etc.) for their country. Have students look around and decide what is best to use for money.

Some questions students should consider in designating something as money:

- Does it "store value" (doesn't rot, like a banana would)?
- Is it easy to recognize and can people agree on its value (does a long pencil = a short one?)?
- Is it easy to carry around?
- Can you make change with it?

Have students compare their choices. What are the advantages and disadvantages of each choice?

Follow-up Questions/Discussions

- Did most people choose something as money that also had a practical use (e.g., a pencil) or something only useful as money (pieces of paper)? What are the advantages and disadvantages of each?
- Why do you think cultures moved from trading things (**barter**) to using money?
- What happens if you choose as currency something that there are too many of (paper clips)? What happens to the price of things (**inflation**)?

Social Questions for Students

- Did you choose something as money that was good for yourself (such as something you had a lot of) or good for most people in your classroom/ country (something everyone had)? How do you decide which to go with if you can't find something that does both? What happens if everyone chooses just what's best for them?

- How did you reach compromises? Describe your system of compromise in a paragraph and say whether it would work in other circumstances.

Lesson 2D—Trade-offs Are On!

Key Concepts
cost-benefit trade-off decision-making process
Special Materials/Media
None
Intro Questions/Thoughts for Students

- How do you make decisions? Do you have a method or do you go with your gut?

Activity

Have each student think of an either/or choice they need to make. It can be studying versus video games, whether or not to go to a party, or choosing between two kinds of food. For both options, the students should write out the benefits of choosing each as well as the costs.

Choice A	Choice B
Benefits (what gained) choosing A	Benefits (what gained) choosing B
Costs (consequences) choosing A	Costs (consequences) choosing B

Students then assign a number in each box, 1–10, for how much it makes them feel good (for benefits) or bad (for costs). For both, 1 means it doesn't matter to them at all and a 10 means it matters to them a lot. The number should just be a gut feeling or reaction; no need to heavily weigh it out or consider just the right number.

Students then cross add, adding the *benefits* of A with the *costs* of B as the total for choosing A and adding the *benefits* of B with the *costs* of A for the total for choosing B. Whichever is higher is the one they should consider more.

Follow-up Questions/Discussions

- Does the choice that "won" using the method above comport (agree) with what you thought "in your gut" would win beforehand? If it worked, why do you think it did? If it didn't work, why do you think it did not?

- Do the totals align with how strongly you felt (or how close the decision was)?
- Was there one box that was hard to come up with things to put in? Why was that? Did it have a lower score than the rest? Does that show it was hard to come up with things because it was just not that big a deal for you?
- For the costs, did you have some reasons or items that were more than just "not getting a benefit"? If not, try to come up with some costs that are beyond not getting the benefit (like a consequence down the line) and recalculate.

Social Questions for Students

- Have you ever wanted to tell a friend something but weren't sure if you should, or maybe try something new, like go out for the play or run for class representative? Try using this system for that kind of decision.
- For social choices, is it sometimes better to not think or weigh things out too long but instead to just do it? What is an example? When is it better to put a lot of thought into making a choice?

Lesson 2E—No More, Please!

Key Concepts

law of diminishing return, marginal utility

Special Materials/Media

sweet soft drink, cookies, candy, or other desired treats

Intro Questions/Thoughts for Students

- Why and when do consumers choose or change what they consume?

Activity

Test subjects (*consumers*) are asked to rate on a scale of 1 to 10 how much they want a cookie or a drink. Whichever one they want more, they are given. After a moment, they are asked again to rate how much they want to consume an additional unit of both items and to consume whichever they rank higher. The test is conducted at least until they switch the product consumed.

Testers make a chart/graph of the numbers (perhaps in conjunction with a math class).

Follow-up Questions/Discussion

- Why did the consumer switch to another product? Why did the score of wanting one more of the thing (called **marginal utility**) go down?

- Did all consumers have the same rate of decrease? Why or why not?
- Does the desire for all products consumed dwindle (**diminishing marginal utility** or the **law of diminishing return**) at the same rate? Would milk and a soft drink decrease at the same rate? Why not? Why do some things "get old fast" but others take longer to get stale (called *varying rates of marginal utility*)?
- Do even fun activities (playing a game, attending a party) get boring after a while?

Social Questions for Students

- Do you ever get tired of being with someone, even someone you like? Is that OK? What can you do or say when this happens? How would you react if a friend told you they needed a break from you for a little bit?

Lesson 2F—There's No Substitute for Your Complements

Key Concepts

substitutes, **complements**, and **accessories**

Special Materials/Media

None

Intro Questions/Thoughts for Students

- Are there any products that you have to have in that form (such as a particular kind of drink), things that have no acceptable replacement if all the stores were out of it?
- Are there any products that you always think of as going together, like peanut butter and jelly?
- Look up the words *compliment* and *complement*; how are the words similar in meaning and how are they different?
- What are **accessories**? What does it mean to *accessorize*?

Activity

The teacher puts the class in groups and then calls out a product, such as "a lawnmower" or "tacos." The groups then have three minutes to work together to come up with a list of **substitutes** and **complements** that are readily available (a goat may or may not be an available substitute for a lawnmower, depending on your community). At the end of time, groups list what they came up with (call them out or write them on the board). Each group gets one point for any substitute or complement not listed by another group (if three groups, 1 point if only one other group had it and 2 points if no other group had it).

For the bonus round, each group then has two minutes to create accessories for the product by creating an inventive, additional companion product that might be sold with the original product (such as an ice-cream maker attachment for the lawnmower that uses the engine to churn or a necktie that squirts hot sauce for tacos).

Follow-up Questions/Discussions

- What kind of products were harder to find substitutes and complements for than others? Was it generally easier to find substitutes or complements? Why do you think that is?
- How many of your accessories were really necessary? Do you think that's also true in real life? Why do manufacturers make so many extra accessories, and why do people buy them? Look at something such as cell phone accessories to see the potential added costs.

Social Questions for Students

- Few products exist without some substitute in most people's lives, but there are "essential" people whom we can't do without (family, friends). Who are yours, and have you thanked them or done something to appreciate them being in your life? Perhaps write a letter to one.
- Whom do you "complement," as in which people do you make better (like jelly to peanut butter)? What can you do to be more of a "complement" to someone? Think of one new person and one way you can complement his or her life, then try to do it!

NOTE

1. See lesson 1A.

Chapter Three

Behavioral Economics

How We Are "Nudged" while Making Our Choices

Let's talk about funerals. We begin the chapter this way for two reasons. First, we want to lay claim to being the first—and possibly only—teacher manual/lesson book to begin a chapter with that sentence. Second, funerals are a great example of the forces of behavioral economics at work.

Considering the matter at hand in regard to a funeral, costs for items such as a casket should be low. Most of such items are a one-time use, and the ultimate user, you should pardon, is not in a position or condition to complain. Yet the average price of a casket is about $2,000 according to the Federal Trade Commission (FTC), with some "high end" ones selling for $10,000! The overall average price of a funeral and burial, according to the FTC, is between $7,000 and $10,000.

So, why do we spend so much? It's hard to justify such costs by the rational factors explained in the last chapter, so we'll have to add new ones, specifically nonrational, emotional motivators such as love, gratitude, and sometimes even guilt. In this case, **"nonrational factors"** is preferable to "irrational factors" as *nonrational* conveys that such factors are *in addition to* the rational ones, rather than negative ones in opposition to rational factors. After all, wanting to spend a lot to show appreciation for a beloved person's final rest appeals to many, if not most, people, and it is exactly that kind of common sentiment that makes so many people responsive to ads that say they will help you in a time of grief or even that one should pre-purchase a plan to save one's children the stress.

All of this talk of funerals (which, we remind you, begins with "fun") is to get a grasp of **behavioral economics**, which takes the neo-classical economics described in the last chapter and broadens the study to include social and psychological factors that influence our economic choices.

The most popular examples of **behavioral** (sometimes called **consumer**) **economics** are the *Freakonomics* books by Steven Levitt. Levitt and his associates show that psychological factors can not only reinforce but even counter rational factors, such as when Israeli day care facilities added a small monetary penalty for parents who picked up their children late. Rather than the added financial punishment acting as a disincentive, decreasing the number of late parents, the charge *increased* the number of late parents as it removed the greater guilt disincentive on the other side of the cost-benefit scales that made some parents rush to pick up their children on time. Such factors become emotional nudges toward a certain choice, whether in the realm of economics or in information selection (such as whom to believe). These nudges can be subtle, subliminal, and perhaps even insidious.

We are more likely to believe our friend's version of how a car accident came to happen rather than a stranger's (unless we know our friend is a bad driver), and we will subconsciously demand more proof from the stranger to be swayed to his version of events. Worst of all, such tacit factors may be known and even utilized by those trying to nudge us in a direction, and unless consumers are aware of such influences by way of media literacy, we will fall prey to it and make choices that are not in our own best interest or are, perhaps, even harmful.

The first step in studying "under the radar"[1] messaging is to realize how much of it we take for granted. We are bombarded with logos, ads, and persuasive messages that may not register consciously. Right now, look up and around; how long did it take you to see a logo or brand name? One well-placed brand name or logo will not cause a complete shift in opinion, but in total such messaging might form our opinions and tastes over time, like the formation of huge cave stalagmites from tiny drops of calcified water over centuries. That is why we repeatedly liken cumulative advertising to the formation of a stalagmite in a cave: drop by drop, almost imperceptibly, it grows, until one day you trip over it.

See Lesson 3A—Count on It

Added to this general effect is that, even while we are aware that we are looking for something definitive that we need (such as food when we are hungry), we may not be self-aware of what we are also emotionally seeking. People are sometimes asked by messengers to do a "gut check" of what they believe or want, but often this is less a request that they should listen to their "gut" so much as become self-aware of the message *they have been listening to already*, like suddenly being quiet and realizing the sounds that have been there the whole time.

When we make choices, it often feels like we are making a decision in that isolated moment, in our "gut," sometimes even saying, "I just want this right now." What we don't see is all of the things that brought us to that moment, including where we see ourselves in the big picture. We bring a lifetime of experiences that we don't remember, such as that teacher who gave out chocolate candy kisses for correct answers or an admired family member who always drove one kind of car. Every one of these quick interactions with a particular seller of a product is called a **brand impression**, and as noted before, they can add up, like the cheer of individual people can combine into a deafening stadium roar.

***See* Lesson 3B—Following the Trail of Breadcrumbs**

We also bring the way we currently see ourselves and let those self-perceptions guide us in choosing. If a girl sees herself as an athlete, she will automatically tune in to sports-related ads. If a boy feels his identity is tied to a certain group (like being a Texan or a skater), ads and other messages that include or appeal to his groups will get noticed, especially if they utilize a kind of character (a **persona**) or include a spokesperson his group would relate to or admire.

Finally, ads and messaging in general don't just appeal to the people we have been, but who we want to be now and in the future. We all want to be better people, so a message that buying a product or siding with one view of a debate makes you "a better you" has a gut appeal that is hard to ignore.

***See* Lesson 3C—I Want You to Want Me!**

***See* Lesson 3D—Spokesperson**

THE TOOLS OF ECONOMIC PERSUASION

You might think that a seller attempting to influence so many potential customers into choosing his product might have to use massive and obvious tools, but in fact it is quite the opposite. We'll address noncommercial persuasive tools later, but in general subtle "nudging" is more effective than an obvious shove, if only because we consumers aren't always aware of it and therefore put up no guard against it. When you also consider how we come to the decision already predisposed in one direction, it doesn't take much to move us. Finally, it is the repetition (or constant "drip") within the stalagmite effect described above that is the key to persuasion as much as it is the force. Not to get Zen, but a small river current may not seem to be able to move a rock, but a hundred years of small, lapping ripples and that rock will be turned to sand.

The simplest nudge is by words. Take, for example, the power of "new and improved." If it's a product we already lean toward, then we'll certainly want it even more, even if we don't really know how it is better (or even why we need it to be better). There's no end to the compliments a product can give itself, claiming by **hyperbole** (exaggerated statements not meant to be taken literally) that the chewing gum you use today will make you a millionaire adored the world over tomorrow. Hyperbole is not considered a lie as long as a reasonable person wouldn't take it seriously, but then again, who can claim he or she is always a reasonable person, and does such a test even account for the general impression such claims leave us with ("What the heck? Let's give it a try!")?

On the other hand, product claims can be so carefully worded, they promise you a definite "maybe" by use of **hedging**, or subtly limiting or making exceptions to claims. How can you argue with the health effects of a product when its makers definitively claim that ***some*** *studies* ***suggest*** *that there* ***may*** *be a link between using their product and good health*? Just like we discussed with conducting social science experiments, in that a wide and varied number of subjects can, with most-assured probability, show a pattern (catch the hedge in there?), analyzing the adjectives used for different products can (there it is again!) show the most common nudge words by product type.

See **Lesson 3E—Improve Improv**

See **Lesson 3F—It's the Best Hyperbole EVER!**

See **Lesson 3G—Trimming the Hedges**

See **Lesson 3H—A Product without Adjectives Is . . .**

Science and data would seem like eternal objective factors in a cost-benefit analysis because such arguments seem rational and grounded in evidence, especially when numbers are involved, but then again, maybe that presumption is just the kind of blind spot in our thinking that leaves us open to sneak attack (or at least secret nudging).

For more than 125 years, soap users have been persuaded by the Proctor family's claim that their soap is "99 44/100 percent pure," never considering that is an adjective phrase without a noun (pure "soap," which is by definition a mixture? pure chemicals? pure nonspecific nonsense?), but it sounds specifically science-y, so it is accepted without question (except by math teachers who want to reduce the fraction!). When placed next to the words "It floats," it gives the impression that the soap's flotation is proof of pureness rather than by properties of buoyancy (and if you don't believe us, send us any gold you have that is so impure it sinks).

Numbers and the varying systems of mathematics, the very tools of precision and accuracy, can be used for just the opposite. In a practice known as **stacking** (as in stacking the deck), scientific studies or the reports from them are set up to deliver the desired confirmation for the producer who's paying for it. That graph that shows brand A's battery with a life bar twice as big as battery B's? Check out the x and y axes (specifically if their confluence is at 0,0), and you may discover the battery life difference is minimal. That drug that claims it was "the only one proven to be effective"? The fine print tells you it was the only drug the lab tested (one for one!).

Even a simple package deal (**bundling** products into one group price) can be deceiving; sure, you are getting a price break for getting 200 items together (like cable channels), but what if you really only wanted to have 10 of them to watch? Is a discount on 190 channels you don't watch a deal?

Remember our prior discussion of marginal utility? Along those lines, let's assume you are a tennis fanatic, so that the Tennis Channel, by itself, would bring 100 HUs (happiness units, of course!) into your life, all for the stand-alone price of $2 per month. On the other hand, watching golf on the Golf Channel is not your cup of tea, only slightly better than watching paint dry (and at least on the paint drying channel you don't have to wonder why announcers are whisper-commenting), so watching it would bring you 1 HU for $2 a month.

You have plenty of other things you'd rather spend those dollars on, but the cable company bundles the two channels together and says you must get them both as the Ultimate Sports Package, though at the discount price of $3.75. A deal? Not really, as you have to pay $1.75 more for something you want to get because the seller is throwing in something you won't use (and on top of it all, you lost enough money to buy a can of tennis balls). That may not seem like a big deal here, but multiply that by a couple of hundred (or consider the standard features thrown in "for free" on a car), and pretty soon we're talking about a lot of court rental fees or even a new racquet (because, in the end, it's always the racquet's fault).[2]

THE VISION QUEST

What is the most dominant of our five human senses (leave it for the students to say "spider")? Many experts say the sense of smell is *often* (there's a hedge again; see how they creep in?) the most linked with memory, but until smell-o-vision becomes a thing, it's not important for electronic advertising, and neither is taste or touch. That pretty much brings marketing down to sight and sound as the primary avenues for commercial persuasion, and of those two, by far, marketers try to earn your dollars more through your eyes than your ears.

Vision is not only the main path of convincing someone, it is the overrider. No doubt we've all seen a movie where someone is forced to lie but tries to override their spoken words with visual cues (like saying no while vigorously nodding yes, or saying they've "seen nothing" while using their eyes to direct a person to look somewhere in particular).

If visual nudging has always been important in advertising, it is more so today than it was one hundred years ago when magazine ads first flourished after the turn of the last century. With fewer avenues for information (and entertainment), ads back then were meant to be carefully read and considered after catching a person's eye. Today, with so many competitors vying for a person's attention—whether in print or online—an ad must have the visual appeal, called "pop" or **eye candy**, to catch us in an instant and hold us long enough for a message to stick before we turn the page or click on the next link. Thus, the very composition of ads has changed to meet our shortness of attention and time.

See Lesson 3I—Single-Frame Storytelling

Specific visual cues, such as a spokesperson wearing a lab coat, tell us immediately she is an expert and therefore anything she says must be scientifically valid. Going more abstract, placing a product amid a pleasing visual, such as a sine curve, can make the viewer look longer and feel more attuned to the ad. Even getting the customer into the brick-and-mortar store isn't always enough; customers may need that extra nudge to seal the deal and buy, so store and restaurant owners try to make their establishments visually appealing if not consumption-stimulating.

See Lesson 3J—Lab Coat Lab

See Lesson 3K—Sine of the Times

Of course, the most central visual cue for a company is its **logo**, or symbol. The word logo is short for logogram, meaning a sign in place of a word (like a peace sign). Companies like to use them because they are easier to see and recognize.

Think of traveling along the highway, looking for a place to eat. You could try to read the names of the restaurants to see if you should pull off, but a quick glance at the golden arches tells you what's there in an instant so you don't miss the exit, plus the visual hits you in your (hungry) gut. Companies spend lots of money on logos, and the ones that work best are the ones you can recognize even out of context. Of course, the logo is not effective unless it is placed where people look, but advertisers study that as well. They have an even better awareness of where the potential buyers are looking than the consumers themselves.

See Lesson 3L—Loco Logo Bingo

In addition to what we see affecting our judgments in ads, *how* we see it can nudge us to certain conclusions. You might think that a marketer can only decide *what* we see, but we still control our viewing perspective. Consider this, though: if we look up to people we admire, down on people we judge, and level with people with whom we empathize, can an ad make us do that?

As investigated at Stanford University many years ago, the right camera angle of an ad can place us in just such a perspective. It can also plop us in the midst of the scene, like we are at the party or up close and personal with food about to be eaten, or it can place us as a removed observer to judge whether we approve or not. We are sitting on our couch, but we are being taken for a virtual ride through ad perspectives!

See Lesson 3M—A View to a Sale

See Lesson 3N—In or Out?

CHAPTER 3 ACCOMPANYING LESSONS

Lesson 3A—Count on It

Key Concepts

media affecting point of view, ubiquity of media, **viral advertising**

Special Materials/Media

None

Intro Questions/Thoughts for Students

- How aware are you of when someone is trying to send you a message to influence your decisions? Do you think you catch more than 50 percent?
- How many ads do you think you are exposed to every day?

Activity

Have students choose a day to carry around a tally sheet. From the moment they wake up (writing down the time), have them record each logo or ad they see or hear as well as the time and manner (billboard, friend's shirt, etc.). How soon before they have seen or heard ten ads? Count seeing logos or hearing the brand name as an ad. Have students make a prediction beforehand as to the time it will take or how many brands they will encounter before noon. Twenty? Fifty? More in a whole day?

Students should include in their count and pay particularly close attention for when people mention a brand name, such as “I went to Starbucks this morning,” or “Have you heard the new tune from . . . ,” or are wearing a shirt or other clothing with a name or logo you can see. This is called **viral advertising** and, in effect, is getting the consumers to be advertisers for the product.

Follow-up Questions/Discussions

- Who had the most? Did anyone get ten before they left their bedroom? Did you take notice of any you weren’t really aware of before?
- Do you think being exposed to that many ads has an effect? Can advertising be in a way like the air we breathe, invisible but all around us and having an effect on us? If you see (or hear) an ad, but you don’t take conscious notice of it, does it still have an effect?
- Some of the ads you encountered seemed accidental (such as driving by), but is it really an “accident” or was it placed there to wait for you and others to pass by and see it, like a highway road sign?
- How many of your tallies were from other people mentioning a brand or wearing it or referring you to an ad (**viral advertising**)? Do you think companies try to encourage this? How many brands do *you* advertise for? Some companies have actually paid kids to secretly promote their products by using them or mentioning them to their friends. Would you be willing to secretly try to sell things to your friends (pretend you like something you don’t) for money?
- Why do you think companies give away free stuff (with their name and logo on it)?
- How does all the advertising we see create a “stalagmite effect?” In what case would this “drip, drip” strategy work on people and when would it not? Could it influence you?

Social Questions for Students

- Can other invisible things around us have an effect, like moods, attitudes, or ways we treat each other? Can being positive or negative toward something (like school) or treating a person a particular way become “normalized” and thus expected of everyone? What if you heard all day that “John is a bad guy”? Might it eventually become your view of him? What can you do?
- A philosopher (Voltaire) once said, “No snowflake in an avalanche ever feels responsible.” What do you think he meant by that?

Lesson 3B—Following the Trail of Breadcrumbs

Key Concepts

brand impression, personal identification with a brand

Special Materials/Media

None

Intro Questions/Thoughts for Students

- When we choose a brand while shopping, do we choose it at that moment or has it been there waiting for us to find at the end of a trail we've been following for a long time, even before we were shopping? When we go into a decision-making (buying) situation, how much of the decision has already been made?

Activity

Every student is given a piece of paper. The teacher (or leader) calls out a product (like "candy bars" or "cars"). Everyone writes down the first three brands that come to mind without thinking too long about it (they should go with their "gut") and then compares.

As a further exercise, everyone writes a quick paragraph (or discusses) after thinking about: "Based on my personality, if I were a soft drink (or car), I would be a _____."

Compare to see if there is a consensus as to a brand's "personality."

Follow-up Questions/Discussions

- Were any brands particularly popular in making lists of three? Besides the product's qualities, why do you think that brand name is at the front of the line? Would another class/school/neighborhood have a different list of most popular?
- Do you think the items at the top of most people's quick-think lists have an advantage in selling? Why? What are the most common factors that determine whether a product makes someone's top three (besides quality)? What do companies do to get their product in this set? How early in your life did this evoked set start to form, and how often do you think the list changes?
- Do companies try to give their product a personality? Look at ads (TV, magazine, or Internet) to see if there are hints about the "personality" they want their product to have.

Social Questions for Students

- If the class is grouped by common answers, are there any people together who aren't normally friends or who don't hang out together? Any "opposite personalities" together? Any other surprises ("I didn't know you liked that, too")? What does that tell you about quick or simple labels for people?

Lesson 3C—I Want You to Want Me!

Key Concepts

packaging yourself (**self-branding**), creating a **persona** in buying and selling

Special Materials/Media

Internet

Intro Questions/Thoughts for Students

- Often, in order to select something like a school, camp, program, and later college, we try to see if the program suits our own character or **persona** (personality or character shown to others). Space camp can make some feel like they were born to be there, as might a sports or arts camp, church program, or school that seems to have the same interests and values, or "personality," as we do. Camps and programs try to get you to try them by creating a persona and then saying, "If you're like us, try us out."
- How can you tell when a program matches your self-perceived persona? What clues do programs put in their brochures, ads, and other messages to indicate what their persona is?

Activity

Students should go to a prospective program's website and analyze what the program is saying about itself and how it communicates its persona. Look for

- the words they use, especially adjectives, that indicate their persona;
- the activities they show and what the pictures portray without words;
- a symbol or logo that sums up their persona; and
- the kind of people they show participating.

Be sure to look at camera angles (majestically looking up, looking down, or eye level), pace (fast action or slow and focused), music, and other production values to get the full effect. Students can then present to the class.

Follow-up Questions/Discussion

- What is the kind of person this program wants? How do you know?
- What is it that makes you think this program fits your persona or does not?
- Can the appeal be "trying too hard," showing too much of just one thing, or showing it too intensively?
- How important is it that you see people like you (that you identify with) participating in the program? If the pictures were of people very different from yourself in age, gender, even race or ability, would that affect your opinion of the program?
- As a follow-up, have the students pretend they are advertising for their class and make a promotional skit (or video) to entice others to come join them.

Social Questions for Students

- If you were to make an accurate video of your peer group, what would it look like?
- What if you made a "sales" video about yourself for such programs (or for your teacher next year to let her know who you are)? What would be your persona? How would you show that?

Lesson 3D—Spokesperson

Key Concepts
ethos in persuasion, endorsement as persuasion
Special Materials/Media
Access to the Internet
Intro Questions/Thoughts for Students

- When you choose to buy or do something, how much are you influenced by famous or admired people selling or doing it? Do you think it works as an influencing technique?
- What kind of people influence your decisions? Do you listen more to athletes? Entertainers? Wise elderly people? Why?

Activity

Find an ad where a famous person is shown using or **endorsing** (promoting) a product or service. For that ad, answer the following:

- Who is the spokesperson, and why are they famous?

- What is the product the person is endorsing?
- Is the product connected (such as sports equipment with an athlete) or unrelated (a soft drink with an athlete) to why the spokesperson is famous?
- Who are the spokesperson's admirers who might be persuaded to try the product?
- Who are the people outside the targeted group (such as fans of a rival team)?
- Does the spokesperson make *you* more interested in the product? Why or why not?

Follow-up Questions/Discussions

- People say they are not influenced, but how many ads did you immediately think of with a famous spokesperson without even researching? Could that be another reason to use a spokesperson?
- Organize the spokespeople by categories, such as sportspeople, entertainers, politicians, or scientists. Are there any overwhelming categories? Why do you think there might be more entertainers endorsing products than scientists? Does this say something about how much we value science? What kind of product could Einstein endorse?
- Are you more persuaded by a famous spokesperson endorsing a product or if the product is endorsed by someone like you (such as an ad with a young person you don't know)? Does it depend on the kind of product?

Social Questions for Students

- Are there "trendsetters" in your school or group? Are there people whom others follow? How did they get that authority?
- What could you endorse that people might consider because you are recommending it? Have each person make an ad in which he or she is the spokesperson for his or her area of "expertise."

Lesson 3E—Improve Improv

Key Concepts

product improvement, ergonomics (designing products and systems to be most efficient for human use)

Special Materials/Media

None

Intro Questions/Thoughts for Students

- What does it mean to "improve" a product?

- Is a product that is “more” or “new” always better? When you hear that a product that’s been out for a while has been redone as “new,” do you automatically assume it is improved or better?
- When a product is said to be “new” or “improved,” does it always mean the product or can it mean the packaging?
- What is ergonomics?

Activity

The class is divided into groups. Taking turns, the teacher (or another group) calls out an everyday product (from pencils to cars). The team called upon then has two minutes to come up with a thirty-second ad they will act out that shows how the product has been redesigned or changed to be “new” or “improved.” The teacher can decide if the improvement must be realistic or fantastical.

Follow-up Questions/Discussions

- How many of the improvements would you consider to be an actual improvement, rather than a change for change’s sake?
- Can a company change a product too much? Might some people miss the old version? Are there any products (such as games) where you like an older version better? Research the story of “New Coke” by the Coca-Cola company.
- Why do companies look to constantly upgrade and improve their product? If they have a winner, why change it?
- In the computer world, there always seem to be “upgrades.” In computer games, there always seem to be add-ons one can buy. Why do you think companies do this, rather than sell all of it at once or wait until they can sell it all as a whole new product?

Social Questions for Students

- In what areas do you feel the need to always improve yourself? Why? Is it more for internal desire or because other people (such as parents) are telling you to improve? Is there a difference in motivation for you?
- When is something you do “good enough”? When is it healthier to stop trying to improve and just enjoy where you are?

Lesson 3F—It’s the Best Hyperbole EVER!

Key Concepts

use of **hyperbole** in advertising

Special Materials/Media

Access to Internet

Intro Questions/Thoughts for Students

- What is *hyperbole*?
- How can you tell when someone is exaggerating to make a point versus trying to lie? Is it the hardest things to do *ever*?

Activity

Have students look for ads that use hyperbole. Look for ads that say "the best" or make claims like "more room than on the moon," for example. Kids should also look for visual hyperbole, such as overreactions of joy or hair standing on end. The examples can be cut out and made into the best hyperbolic collage *ever*!

Follow-up Questions/Discussion for Students

- What kinds of products use hyperbole more than others?
- Is there a difference between general hyperbole ("the Greatest Show on Earth") and directed hyperbole ("a million times better than our competitor, brand X")?
- Were the hyperboles used more for humor or bragging? If people know that hyperbole is not true, why use it as a tool? Why is it still effective?
- Were there any hyperboles that you were unsure if they might be true? Do you think, over time, hyperbole can come to be accepted as true? Should there be a rule or test as to what kind of hyperbole can be used?

Social Questions for Students

- What kinds of things do you possibly exaggerate about yourself or your life? Is that OK?
- Can someone come to believe their own exaggerations after a while?
- Do some people like to exaggerate bad things in their lives as well as good things? Why would someone do that?
- Is it OK to take pride in something you do, even if you are not the best one at it? When is it better to be honest, even if it means admitting you're not the best at something?

Lesson 3G—Trimming the Hedges

Key Concepts

hedging as a marketing tool, use of **indefinite pronouns** for hedging claims

Special Materials/Media

Access to Internet, highlighter (or ability to copy and highlight/print)

Intro Questions/Thoughts for Students

- Have you ever heard a sentence that sounds sure and definite, but the more you think about it, it's not as specific as you once thought? We can say, "I want the red ball," but what if there are five balls of different shades of red?
- What are an **indefinite pronouns**? How are they used? Can they be misused or poorly used?

Activity

Look for ads that seem to make definite statements but have indefinite words that limit the statement in some way:

- indefinite pronouns (*many, few, some*)
- hedging adjectives (*some, most*)
- hedging adverbs (*mostly, partially, mainly, often, sometimes, usually*)
- mitigating introductory verbs (*seems to, appears to, tends to, suggests, might*)
- disclaimers (*results not typical, genuine faux leather*[3])

For these sentences, copy or print them and then highlight the limiting (hedging) words. Take turns reading aloud the sentences, first without the hedges and then with the hedges. Discuss how the hedging words change the meaning of the sentence.

As an alternative to ads, students can look at daily horoscope predictions and highlight definite statements ("you will win the lottery") in one color and hedges ("chances are good," "the odds are in your favor . . . ," "someone you know") in another.

Follow-up Questions/Discussions

- How much do the hedging words change the meaning? If you think of sales ads as a promise of what the product will do, how firm a promise are you getting with hedged sentences?

- Why do you think sellers add these hedge words? Are some more effective than others?
- Do customers read these sentences as closely as you do? As a follow-up experiment, show pictures of the ads to people, ask them to look at an ad with hedging for fifteen seconds, and then ask them what the product does. See how many respondents say the promise as a definite statement. Do you think advertisers know that many of the hedges are not noticed?

Social Questions for Students

- Have you ever hedged an answer, such as whether you will be at a party or if you did a chore? Why did you do so?
- Have you ever hedged your thoughts to play it safe ("I'm probably wrong, but . . ." or "This is just a guess, but . . .")? Why did you do this? When is this good to do and when is it counterproductive to voicing your ideas?
- If you are hedging and the listener gets the wrong idea, is that a form of lying?
- How careful are you to pick up on hedging language when hearing or making promises ("I'll try")? What does that do to a promise? Is it better to make a promise absolute?

Lesson 3H—A Product Without Adjectives Is . . .

Key Concepts
use of adjectives in advertising
Special Materials/Media
Access to Internet
Intro Questions/Thoughts for Students

- Advertisers use adjectives as a way to describe their product, but are there certain adjectives that go with product types (like "durable" for jeans or "soft" for toilet paper)? Is this planned or is it just the qualities we have come to expect of certain products?

Activity

Divide up the class by product categories, such as breakfast cereals, luxury cars, women's clothing, and sports drinks (or any other you wish). This also can be done by taking one product, such as clothing, and dividing it by types: men's, women's, sport, dressy, children's, and so on. Each group is to watch at least ten ads for their products and write down all the adjectives used to describe that product and the number of times the word is used. Together, the class can create a chart:

Products:	
Most common adjective (#)	
Second most common (#)	
Third most common (#)	
Fourth most common (#)	

Have the class look for patterns. Were they surprised by any words? Try mixing the words to see if they could apply to another product (like "crunchy" from cereal to a car). As an improv exercise, draw a random product and a random adjective and have the students in groups design an ad that blends the two.

Follow-up Questions/Discussions

- Why do advertisers use the same words for the same products? Is it lack of imagination or that we expect certain products to have certain qualities? Would you think less of a product if it didn't have the usual word with it (like "safe" for medicine)?
- For fun, each group should make up a new adjective for their product, a word that describes something that is generally true but has no adjective yet (like *anti-soggish* for cereal that doesn't get soggy too fast in milk).

Social Questions for Students

- Are there adjectives that are commonly used to describe you? If you could have any adjective accurately describe you in five years, what would you want that adjective to be?

Lesson 3I—Single-Frame Storytelling

Key Concepts
visual ads as suggesting stories
Special Materials/Media
Access to Internet
Intro Questions/Thoughts for Students

- Comic strips and comic books tell a story in several pictures, but can an entire story be told in a single picture? Often, ads drop you in the middle of a situation (such as a messy house but with a sparkling clean kitchen floor and a happy homeowner with a mop and Mr. Clean). You can figure out a lot of the background story (the kitchen was messy before, perhaps after making a big holiday meal, but was cleaned up easily) along with the ad's text (ad copy) that often adds to the narrative.

Activity

Have students find an ad that seems to drop the viewer into a situation. Students should then write a paragraph that tells the story of the ad as a problem-and-solution format. Alternatively, students can use Gustav Freytag's historic five-part structure of a story to describe what is depicted in an ad:

- ***Exposition***—story setup (There once was a man who wanted to have people over for a party . . .).
- ***Rising Action***—path to a problem (. . . but his floors and bathrooms were dirty . . .).
- ***Climax***—peak of the problem or turning point (. . . with only minutes until the guests would arrive, he grabbed the instant cleaner . . .).
- ***Falling Action***—resolving the problem (. . . and he miraculously cleaned his house in time . . .).
- ***Resolution***—afterward/happily ever after (. . . and his guests were impressed at how neat he was).

Follow-up Questions/Discussion

- Will two people seeing the same ad always see the same story? Are most of the stories built around a theme (such as problem-solution)? Who or what are the heroes of the ads?
- You can also look for two-picture ads that convey before/after or the perfect ideal and then the reality (usually wanting) and have students explain what happened between the two as a lesson in cause-effect and deductive reasoning.

Social Questions for Students

- How well can you estimate what another person is feeling just by looking at their expression? There are some online tests;[4] see if you can use them to correctly identify emotions by facial expressions.

- Great photography also drops you in the middle of a story. Look up the photos of Dorothea Lange, a famous photographer during the Great Depression. For one of her pictures (or someone else's), write a story about what happened to the people and what they are thinking. Being able to understand another's feelings, even by a picture, is called *empathy*.

Lesson 3J—Lab Coat Lab

Key Concepts
visual appeal to authority
Special Materials/Media
lab coat (part 2)
Intro Questions/Thoughts for Students

- What does an "expert" or smart person look like to you? Is that always true?
- When we hear something, do we use the way the speaker is dressed to help decide if what we hear is believable? Are we more likely to listen to people who look like "experts"?

Activity

Have students look for ads that have people (especially spokespeople) dressed in lab coats or as doctors. Also look for settings and props that imply "science" (such as a lab or a microscope). By making a chart that shows the trends, students should keep track of what kind of product it is and what's being said about the product when they show such people or sets.

Follow-up Questions/Discussions

- Which products commonly showed "science" people or sets? Why do you think that is?
- Are the statements more believable because they are said by a science-looking person or in a science setting? Try imagining everyday people (or kids) making the same statements. Does it sound as believable even if it is the same information?
- For a fun follow-up, pick a product that doesn't have a lot of science references in its ads (like pencils or candy bars). Make an ad that implies a lot of scientific research and testing went into making it (you might be surprised how much research actually does go into virtually every product).

Social Questions for Students

- How often do you believe or follow someone because they just naturally seem to know what they are talking about or seem to assume leadership?
- Are some people believed more because they "look smart"? How about the people who don't "look the part"? What are the consequences of each of these scenarios?

Lesson 3K—Sine of the Times

Key Concepts
visual cues as setting mood, aesthetics
Special Materials/Media
magazine ads
Intro Questions/Thoughts for Students

- Are there any shapes or forms that are pleasing to people more than others? Do you think more people like hard angles or soft curves?
- Do you think people creating ads use abstract lines and shapes to catch viewers' eyes and give a picture appeal?

Activity

Draw out a sine curve for your class and explain what it is and (if done in coordination with an Algebra I class) how it is derived:

Ask students what the curve reminds them of (or where they see it in nature), such as ocean waves. The soft curve can be contrasted with a harsher, pointier oscillation.

Ask students which one appeals to them more and why. Students can look around the room for examples of such curves (either one "hump" or the double curve, stretching horizontally or vertically). Now have students look for sine curves in ads. Again, it can be a single curve or double, horizontally or vertically oriented, one color or multiple. Students can create a collage of sine curves in ads.

Follow-up Questions/Discussions

- For what kinds of products did you find sine curves? Were there a lot for one kind of product?
- Did the sine curves imply anything, like smoothness or ease? How can you tell?
- Were there any "hidden" or naturally occurring sine curves? Look at pictures of the back of an unsaddled horse or ocean waves; is there a sine curve there? Where else might such a curve be hidden?
- Why do you think there are a lot of curves in advertising? Are such curves placed there to make us feel "in tune" with the ad, or could it be that they were not put in intentionally, but just like the consumers, people who design the ads are naturally drawn to the curves and put them in *subconsciously* (done without being aware they are doing it)? Do you think we see them simply because we are looking for them?

Social Questions for Students

- Is there a possible problem with being drawn to or pushed away from things for reasons we are not consciously aware of?
- Do you like people or things better if they seem familiar to you and, conversely, don't like things that seem different or strange? What are good reasons to do this (safety) and what are possible downsides (missing out on a new experience)?

Lesson 3L—Loco Logo Bingo

Key Concepts
company logos, **brand impression**
Special Materials/Media
Internet, possible mall visit
Intro Questions/Thoughts for Students

- Why do companies (and other institutions) use logos? How many do you know?
- How did you come to know all the logos you know? If it wasn't a conscious effort, how did you learn all the logos?
- Do you know of any logos for products you have never bought? How about for products you are not allowed to buy (such as alcohol)?

Activity

Students look on the Internet, compiling logos without the company name, and then test each other on how many they know. Students then make a 5 X 5 bingo square and choose which logos they want to put in and where. Students then watch and write in the date and time they see the logo in person or in advertising (an actual store doesn't count). See who gets bingo (or blackout) first!

Follow-up Questions/Discussion

- Besides stores and products you buy, what else has logos? Sports teams? What is your school's logo? How does it make you feel to see a car with your school's logo (or a rival school's)?
- Why do you think you know logos for things you can't buy, such as alcohol? Is having you know these logos done on purpose by companies selling these products?

Social Questions for Students

- Is there a difference between well-known and popular?
- Is it always good to be the most well-known? When could that be a bad thing?
- What might be the downside of always being known/recognized?

Lesson 3M—A View to a Sale

Key Concepts
visual perspective of ads
Special Materials/Media
Access to Internet
Intro Questions/Thoughts for Students

- How does virtual reality work? How does it make you see things from a certain perspective when you are staying still? Can ads do that?

Activity

Students are to find three kinds of ads:

1. Ads where the viewer (student) is looking up at the spokesperson or scene

2. Ads where the viewer (student) is looking on an even level at the spokesperson or scene
3. Ads where the viewer (student) is looking down on the spokesperson or scene

After collecting the ads as a class, look at each group to determine:

- the pattern of ads using that view and
- how the class thinks the viewer is supposed to feel about what is depicted.

Follow-up Questions/Discussions

- Generally, we look up at people we admire, such as a leader speaking to us (for a historical tie, have students look up the history of a *rostrum* and what it has to do with Rome, sea warfare, and ships!). When we look even with someone, we empathize with them, like we could be in his or her place. When we look down on someone, we are judging him or her, usually for the worse. How are ad makers using these perspectives (and presumably, your mood) to help nudge you to make a decision in their favor?
- How many (or what percentage) of the ads were positive about their own product, how many were negative about another's product (or displayed a negative "don't be like this" situation), and how many were neutral? Why do you think that is?
- Besides ads selling products, who else might use virtual perspective? Look at ads for politicians to see what perspectives they use. Why do you think they do this?

Social Questions for Students

- Can you communicate approval or disapproval of something without words? Act out a conversation, once with a person giving silent approval and once with silent disapproval.
- Would you consider yourself a judgmental person? Is it possible for you to judge someone without even knowing you are doing so?

Lesson 3N—In or Out?

Key Concepts
visual perspective of ads
Special Materials/Media
Access to Internet
Intro Questions/Thoughts for Students

- If you are being introduced to a new activity, such as a game or sport, would you rather jump right in or watch on the side for a moment to figure it out? What are the advantages of both approaches? How does each way make you feel about the activity?

Activity

Students look for ads that either:

- convey a sense that the viewer (student) is in the middle of the action, such as the people in the ad are looking right at them, the food is "in your face" about to be eaten, or any other way "you are there"; or
- convey the idea that you are removed, such as looking from afar, looking up or down (as opposed to level), or looking at the picture somehow inset with a border or frame (so it's a picture of a picture).

To make it a game, have the students gather in groups, and the teacher calls out either "in" or "out" plus a type of product ("food" or "game"). Students then try to see who the first group is to find an ad of that kind relating to that product.

Follow-up Questions/Discussions

- Did you find more "ins" or "outs"? How did they relate to certain products?
- Why do "in" ads or "out" ads work better with some products than others?

Social Questions for Students

- How do you decide which activities to be "in" and which to be "out"? How do you strike a good balance? Make a list of activities you like to be "in" and which you like to be "out" (observe). Do you think you have a good balance in your life? If not, what can you do?
- Is there any problem with being always "in" or always "out"?
- Many people say that, looking back at school, they regret more being out of school activities than being in one in which they were not successful. Why do you think that is?

NOTES

1. "Under the radar" messaging is generally designed so as not to be noticed directly, or so the receiver isn't aware they are receiving messaging from professionals. For example, a marketing firm might hire teens to promote a brand to other teens so it seems nonscripted, peer

to peer. Depending on your point of view, this is either an ingenious or insidious form of marketing.

2. Many consider the McDonald's Happy Meal, rolled out in 1979, the granddaddy of modern bundling, combining the low-profit burger with the much higher-profit fries and a drink.

3. "Faux" is French for false or fake, but many people aren't aware of that. *Quelle dommage!*

4. See, for example, https://socialintelligence.labinthewild.org/mite/, https://well.blogs.nytimes.com/2013/10/03/well-quiz-the-mind-behind-the-eyes/, or https://greatergood.berkeley.edu/quizzes/ei_quiz/take_quiz.

Chapter Four

Coolness

The Super Nudge

We don't want to speak on behalf of all those involved in behavioral economics and media literacy, but there is a certain irony in the profession, for we are compelled to study "coolness" in all its forms more than perhaps any other academic discipline, yet we, as a group, were probably the folks with whom coolness least intersected in our formative years! So far, we've looked at various tools (or tricks) for nudging consumers toward a particular choice in their seemingly "independent" decision making. The fact is, however, no other tool comes with more attachments, no trick is more potent, than using the idea of something being "cool" to nudge people in its direction.

To understand coolness, let's go back to the late 1800s to a man with a cool name, **Thorstein Veblen**. Unfortunately for Veblen, he sacrificed any such coolness by studying philosophy and then economics. At that time, nascent economics would have stressed that a person purchases a product based purely on its utility, or usefulness, and that such a person would consider the product's utility in light of price and quality in making his decision, a very rational think-through on all accounts.

Now, imagine Veblen, trained in this economic mindset, sitting in a park, watching the people stroll by, when he sees and considers a well-dressed, able-bodied man strolling by with a well-appointed, highly polished walking stick. To Veblen's eye, the man is not in need of a walking stick, as he seems fit. So why then did this man of industry carry and, more to the point, purchase a cane? Without utility, the price and quality factors do not even matter. The man is apparently of a sound mind and by his appearance seems successful in making financial decisions, as do many other wealthy men like him who eagle-eyed Veblen has now noticed have also purchased walking sticks.

What then could be the reason for this? Undaunted by the confining walls of considering only sensible factors in decision making, our superhero economist Veblen the Vanquisher breaks through the boundaries of neoclassical economics to eventually come to the conclusion that the purchase was not done for a conscious, rational reason but for a conscious, *nonrational* one: to impress others. By utilizing a walking stick he does not need, our stroller sends the signal, not only that his hands are free from labor to do as he pleases with them, but that he can afford to spend his money on unnecessary, ostentatious items.

Veblen coins a term for this kind of act, **conspicuous consumption**, in his seminal 1899 book *The Theory of the Leisure Class* and with this, in effect, launches the study of nonrational economic decision making (though to date the glory of being immortalized as an action figure still eludes him).

One could say that Veblen is the first to study the idea of doing things to be cool, but that motivation, even according to Veblen, has been around a lot longer. Going well back before Veblen, say about ten thousand years, to the dawn of civilization, let's consider two rival tribes called the *crunchies* and the *smoothies*. They both covet peanuts as a food source (yes, the divide probably goes back that far), so the crunchies attack the smoothies and take their peanuts.

In the ensuing battle, one crunchy warrior, Jiffy, finds the ceremonial eating spoon of the king of the smoothies, so he takes it. Being part of the captured goods, it is what people (notably pirates) called *booty*. The spoon has no practical use. It is too big and heavy, but Jiffy wants to keep it to show off what he captured so his fellow tribesmen will admire him. Veblen calls such an item **Honorific Booty**, or a thing acquired for the utility of admiration or feeling good about having it, i.e., it's cool.

We can take this one step further, subdividing such goods into two kinds: **Internal Honorific Booty**, or things that make us feel good for having them regardless of who knows (your *Lord of the Rings*–like "precious"), and **External Honorific Booty**, or the things that make us feel good because others see us with it and admire us for having it.

See **Lesson 4A—But What You Don't Know . . .**

See **Lesson 4B—But What I Need You to Know . . .**

Personal, long-term satisfaction may come more from Internal Honorific Booty (especially when the things you possess are nontangibles like happiness, a sense of belonging, giving to others, and a sense of self), but it's External Honorific Booty that most often leads to what society deems "cool" (at least on the surface). In fact, an old synonym for cool (that actually predates it) is ***panache***. Panache means having a style or manner that stands out (for admiration), but its etymology (linguistic history) is the giveaway. Panache comes from an old French word that meant a plume or ostrich feather that French military officers wore on their hats. Why did they wear such gaudy things? It was a privilege of rank, to stand apart from one's own nonofficer troops (to say "respect me") and to stand out to the enemy, fellow aristocratic officers (perhaps to say, "Hey, don't hurt me; just take me prisoner and we'll talk"). That's what coolness got you back in the day!

Today, we don't wear plumes to stand out, but we wear many things to be cool, from certain labels to facial expressions and airs of attitude. We like to be seen in certain places, in certain ways, and with certain people. We know, rationally, that being near admired things doesn't make us better people, but who can resist that irrational pull to try to appropriate some admiration or have some coolness rub off?

Coolness would seem to be something the people decide, whether by collectively admiring and imitating someone with "it" (as was said of Clara Bow a century ago), attaching themselves to a consensus cool item (like Ray-Ban Wayfarers for sixty years), or joining in a movement or cultural vibe (the preppy look of the 1980s).

Along with the people's choice, however, has come a host of marketers trying to "catch the wave" of emerging new trends (called **coolhunting**) and then trying to influence, in turn, what is deemed cool by consumers. Along the way, marketers also discovered that one of the most powerful cool-nudgings is not just playing up the positiveness of being part of the cool but preying on the fear of isolation if one did not do so and was then left out.

See Lesson 4C—Fad All Over

One of the stranger aspects of cool is that cool kills itself. As soon as everyone is doing it, it no longer has that stand-out panache, and coolness has to move on to something else. Veblen referred to the process as **pecuniary emulation**, whereby the lower, less-monied classes imitate the wealthier ones' tastes and choices as best they can, which eventually drives the wealthy to find a new source of panache.

A wealthy person may have a limousine and driver; while below them a person might have a Bentley or other rare, high-end car but drive it themselves; below that a luxury car, then a mid-level car, economy car, down to economics teachers taking scooters to work! The *Freakonomics* folks similarly have a great study on how girls' names start off among the elite and then are adapted over the years by the lower socioeconomic classes until the upper classes move on. In any case, chasing cool is like chasing your shadow; it's short-lived and gone before you can catch it.

So how do marketers retool what was hip but is now on the downside arc of cool? They will rebrand, reintroduce, or tell you something is new and edgy. If "this ain't your mama's or daddy's" car, root beer, or light bulb, then the implication is it is new and just for you.

Panache can also come from adding to something otherwise ordinary an **affectation**, such as using British (*theatre*) or French (*pointe*) spelling for a name, adding a calculated language flair (*non?*), striking an indifferent attitude (which, of course, must be done in public to demonstrably show your non-caring attitude to those whom you care to see it!), or claiming an exotic origin (such as ice cream created in the Bronx but with a Danish-sounding name or made by a couple of counter-culture guys in Vermont). In the end, coolness comes from panache, and panache has been and always will be about only some people having it, and that may or may not include you (so now you want it!).

See Lesson 4D—Affectation Affection

One particular aspect of cool that really stands out as a powerful nudger is being a rebel. It's a tough line to walk because coolness is about portraying it as a natural, self-inherent trait one has regardless of one's environment, yet being a rebel means being aware of and reactive to one's environment. And if you try too hard, even in rebellion, it isn't cool.

The high point of coolness, then, at least by pop culture standards, is the person who goes her own way, and it just happens to go against society's norms as she won't be confined by them. It's the gal who just shrugs and says, "Sometimes you gotta break the rules" but is not in open defiance; it's just who she is. One imagines that this is more prevalent in America; in more authoritarian countries, one could see the statement "Sometimes you gotta break the rules" in a movie immediately followed by the speaker's demise and then a state official explaining why following the rules is *always* the best and coolest course.

See Lesson 4E—The (Non)Pursuit of Cool

See Lesson 4F—Sometimes Ya Gotta Break the Rules . . .

Truly cool rebels, then, don't shout at the system but walk their own path. They generally don't acquire External Honorific Booty (because that might show a concern for what others think of them), but they might acquire what could be called **Negative Honorific Booty**, or things that society might not like but, because they are an independent trendsetter, they do anyway and then garner admiration and personal pride (like Hippies sporting long hair), at least until they inspire too many others to imitate them and then they have to move on.

Coolhunting, by either consumers or marketers, ends up being exhausting. For the price of quick and ephemeral popular approval, we have to spend lots of brainpower caring about not caring, watching what everyone else does to make sure we do something different to show we aren't affected by the majority. We can waste time, money, and resources, all in an ever-growing competition to outcool each other.

An economist named John Kenneth Galbraith pointed out in 1958 that, for the cost of materials to build one super-stretch limousine, at least two other cars, could be built for two families (and the cars would be more fuel-efficient). Still, that's the price of a predominantly free-market society, and to borrow from Winston Churchill (who was borrowing from someone else), perhaps it's the worst kind of an economy, save for all the others.

Perhaps the answer lies in an old Cold War term, MAD, which back then stood for *mutual assured destruction* and was the idea that either side could blow up the other, so let's just not and chill (and give that chilling the affectation-sounding name *détente*). Today in the battle for coolness, perhaps we should adopt MAD, but this time have it stand for *mutually assured dweebness*: we're all awkward at times; we're all uncool at times; so let's just chill; save the money, time, and effort; and maybe have an ice cream (no matter who makes it or where it's from).

CHAPTER 4 ACCOMPANYING LESSONS

Lesson 4A—But What You Don't Know . . .

Key Concepts

Internal Honorific Booty, **monetary value** versus **sentimental value**

Special Materials/Media

None

Intro Questions/Thoughts for Students

- What gives things "value"?
- What are the things that you value most, regardless of their monetary value? What is **sentimental value**?
- If you were going to help colonize Mars and could only take five things with you (NASA will provide all your necessities), what would they be?

Activity

Students make a list of things that are most valuable to them and why. They should then estimate the monetary value, such as if they were to sell it at a garage sale; how much do they think a stranger would pay for it? Students should also ask the same of their parents and bring in a list of their parents' most valuable possessions, like the Mars question above.

Follow-up Questions/Discussions

- Did the things on your list have more **monetary** or **sentimental value**?
- Were the items valued because they were associated with a person you know or an event in your life or somehow tied to you over a period of time (like a stuffed animal)?
- Were your parents' lists like yours? Were your parents guided by the same motivations as you were in keeping things?
- Without naming it, was there anything on your list you'd rather others not know you have?
- By looking at the entire class's lists of things and the reasons for valuing them, what are the most common nonmonetary motives for people valuing things? Do you think it reflects the way most people think?

Social Questions for Students

- In the long run, what are the things that are important to you? How important is money in achieving them?
- Is money valuable in and of itself or as a means to get other stuff? What does that stuff give you? What's the end goal?
- Does money buy happiness, in your opinion?

Lesson 4B—But What I Need You to Know . . .

Key Concepts

External Honorific Booty, **conspicuous consumption**

Special Materials/Media

Access to Internet

Intro Questions/Thoughts for Students

- What things have value to you in part because you want people to admire you for having these things?
- What things in your life (objects or activities) give you status or make people admire you?
- Do advertisers use the implied pitch "you will be admired" as a sales technique?
- How can you tell when someone is looked up to or admired?

Activity

Students look for ads that promote a product by implying that using the product will earn admiration or respect. It can be other people looking at the user, or it might display the product user standing out in a crowd or in a position of power with the product (see Lesson 3M).

Follow-up Questions/Discussions

- Were there any particular kinds of products that were especially represented in your findings?
- Were there any particular characteristics of the people in the ads benefiting from the product as to gender or age? Was there one kind of lifestyle (partier, business person, retired, etc.) that stood out?
- As a follow-up, pick ordinary objects in the room (like a stapler). Plan and then act out a thirty-second ad that shows a person being admired for having and using the ordinary object.

Social Questions for Students

- Do you admire some people for what they have rather than who they are? Is it admiration or jealousy?
- Do you ever get mad because you think some people get things they do not deserve? What do you do when you feel that way?
- Do you ever have something you want to show off? What about showing off skills as opposed to objects?

Lesson 4C—Fad All Over

Key Concepts

panache, **conspicuous consumption**, **bandwagon effect**, **fads**

Special Materials/Media

Internet, adults for interviewing

Intro Questions/Thoughts for Students

- Did you ever buy or own something in large part because "everyone else" had one or was doing it (like fidget spinners)? Did you ever want something before you even knew what it was because you didn't want to be left out? This is called the **bandwagon effect** and has been around a long time. Do you know of any historical **fads** (intense, temporary interest or popularity in a product or activity) that resulted from a bandwagon effect?

Activity

Students are to interview parents and grandparents and look online for fads that occurred in the past (from dance marathons of the 1930s, to hula hoops in the 1950s, to pet rocks of the 1970s, to the "preppy" look of the 1980s or "grunge" look in the 1990s). The class then constructs a giant wall-sized timeline of the fads, complete with pictures. The class can vote which ones they think they would have tried back then or even try to re-create one (good luck finding a phone booth for phone booth stuffing).

Follow-up Questions/Discussions

- Does it seem like every generation (or decade) has a fad? Why is that?
- Teenagers seem more involved with fads than other age groups. Why do you think that is?
- Do some fads of the past seem silly to you? Do you think people in the future will think yours are silly?
- What is the appeal of spending money on a fad, especially one like pet rocks?
- How do you think marketers try to get their products to be part of a fad? How do they help spread the fad?
- Back in chapter 2, we learned about a product's usefulness or **utility**. Is helping a person to be accepted as part of the in-group a part of a product's **utility**? Should it be? What's it worth in adding to the price?
- Can you think of word or speaking fads? Research some (rhyming in the 1920s was the bee's knees; Hippie words in the 1960s were groovy; Valley girl speak in the 1980s was totally tubular!) and try them out.

Social Questions for Students

- What are the current fads for your group? Are there fads that are particular to your school, area, or even state that are not so much a fad in the rest of the country? How did you learn of the fad?
- Does it make you especially proud if you are one of the first to be part of a fad? Why is that?
- Are there any fads that you would probably not do (wear, participate in) if it was not the "in thing to do"? You are probably not alone, so why do so many still do it?
- What might be the reason someone doesn't join a fad and does something different? What do you think when you see someone who doesn't go by what everyone else is doing?

- If there was a fad that you thought was bad or dangerous, what could you do? What if your friend wanted to try it?

Lesson 4D—Affectation Affection

Key Concepts
Affectation as coolness
Special Materials/Media
Access to the Internet
Intro Questions/Thoughts for Students

- If you hear of a product being from another country, does that make you think it is special or higher quality? What countries do you associate with high quality and for what products?
- If a marketer wants to make their product seem exotic, what can they do with its name?

Activity

Students are detectives, looking for clues locally and on the Internet for places or products that are disguised by having non-English names. They should then determine if the product:

- is truly imported from that country,
- is made locally but is based on another country or culture (such as a restaurant), or
- is made in America but is taking on foreign airs. Note that some products (Häagen-Dazs) are actually American products or are substantially made in America. Others have simple respellings, such as *colour*, *theatre*, or *pointe*. A product can also use pictures on the label or lettering borrowed from another alphabet.

Make a display of products in each category and explain how your research and detective work discovered which were the posers trying to pretend to be exotically foreign. What do you think the product maker's motives were in giving this impression?

Follow-up Questions/Discussion for Students

- Generally, did the exotic products cost more or less than the domestic ones? For goods really made in other countries, why might they cost more? For the ones that only sound foreign, why do you think the price is higher?

- Why do you think certain countries were imitated? Would the product be as appealing if you changed the country it pretends to be from?
- For the products that pretend to be from another country, they state their true, American origin on the back, but do most people read that part? Should there be a law that requires them to say "Product of the USA" on the front in large letters or should people just be careful? Do you read all the labels (especially the back ones) when you buy something (such as ingredients)?
- On the other hand, why might a product claim or pretend to be "made in the USA" when it is made partially or wholly in another country (or many of its parts were)?
- Besides putting on affectations of being from another country or culture, some products pretend to be an upstart "little guy" business when they are owned by a big, mainstream corporation (look at many of the different soft drink brands). Is this an affectation? Why do it?
- For a fun follow-up, choose everyday objects in the classroom (stapler, tape dispenser) and give them exotic names and make a thirty-second ad to sell them.

Social Questions for Students

- Some people call it being a "poser," but how much is it OK to pretend to be something you are not in order to be more popular? Where is the line for people, such as pretending you play a sport you really don't play or saying you have traveled or met famous people you have not? If there is no harm, is there no foul?
- *Embellishment* is adding extra things to a story to make it more entertaining or interesting. When is this OK and when is it not? When a friend tells you about their day? A movie about a historical figure? A witness testifying in court?
- Since we don't have time to constantly check each other's stories, how important is honesty and trust to making a group work? How do we make a Code of Honor, and what things should be in it (what should we promise to not lie or exaggerate about)? Perhaps your class can create a class Honor Code if you do not have one and all sign your names.

Lesson 4E—The (Non)Pursuit of Cool

Key Concepts

passive cool

Special Materials/Media

None

Intro Questions/Thoughts for Students

- Everyone wants to be cool, but how hard should you try to be cool? Can you try too hard to be cool?

Activity

The class should brainstorm "cool characters" on TV shows and in movies. For each, have the students list what makes them cool. Then the students should discuss how much of that coolness comes from the character trying to intentionally *look* cool, rather than the character doing their thing and others saying it's cool. This includes whether the character brags or makes efforts for people to notice their coolness.

After that, kids can look at ads to see how much characters who are cool are, again, just *being* cool (and admired) versus appearing to say, "Look at me." Pay attention to how concerned the cool character is with being seen (or seen as cool), versus people just seeing him that way (look for whether the cool character is looking at the other people or looking off into the distance while being admired).

Follow-up Questions/Discussions

- Are more cool characters actively cool (looking to be seen as cool) or passively cool (just seen that way)?
- Which do you consider cooler, passive cool or active cool? Why?
- How much bragging did you see done by cool characters?
- For the ads, how do the products (according to the marketers) help someone be passively cool? Do you think all the products really work that way? Why or why not?

Social Questions for Students

- Do you know people who "try too hard" to be cool? Some people are social "ducks," meaning they look like they are gliding smoothly above the surface but below the surface they are paddling like crazy trying to stay afloat in the social water. Do you think perhaps more people are ducks than you can tell? What if everyone who seems comfortable is really a bit anxious and scared? Would it make you feel better to know other people are unsure, say at a dance or speaking publicly?
- Perhaps give out index cards for students to *anonymously* indicate how confident they are or even say what their social worry is. If they can be read aloud (anonymously), it might be comforting for students to realize many are anxious about the same things.

Lesson 4F—Sometimes Ya Gotta Break the Rules . . .

Key Concepts
rebellion as coolness
Special Materials/Media
None
Intro Questions/Thoughts for Students

- What does it mean to be a "rebel"? It is usually defined as a person in opposition to a government or rule, but what exactly does one have to rebel against to be one? Does it matter if the purported rebel is going against an unfairness (like people cheating) or something that is generally seen as OK (like obeying traffic lights)?

Activity

For as many movies as students can think of, they should try to identify a character who is a rebel and fill in the chart like the one below.

Movie	Character	Rule or social norm they are rebelling against	How do they rebel?	How is the world better by their rebellion?

Follow-up Questions/Discussions

- Generally, do good guys rebel against bad rules and bad guys rebel against good rules?
- How many movies can you find where the hero followed all the rules and prevailed? If there are few, why is that so? What message is being sent?
- Can you admire a rule breaker who isn't trying to make things better for others but is just motivated because they don't want to obey the rule?
- It almost always turns out OK in the end, but consider other possibilities when the hero breaks a rule. What problems might have arisen? Why was the rule there in the first place? Did the hero think about the people that might get hurt by his breaking the rule (such as driving crazy might lead to a crash)?

Social Questions for Students

- When is it OK to break rules? Look up heroes such as Rosa Parks.
- We think we are the best judge of when rules should be followed, but do you always know the consequences? For example, if you cut class and the

teacher sees you are missing, how many people will be called out to look for you? What if they had important things to do but then had to look for you? How much is a rebel responsible for the "ripple effect" of his or her actions (like the smashed bystander's car in a movie chase)?

- How many people do you rely on *not* to be rebels? What if the people at the power station or the food providers decided to be rebels and not work today?

Chapter Five

Consumer Demographics

Seeking Media Lit's Holy GRAIL

Fun toy cars, a cool shade of eyeliner, and a reclining chair for an afternoon nap. All three are things that large groups of people would want and would pay money for (*consume*), but the members of those groups vary a great deal. Very few products are desired by everyone. Most sellers find they do better if they don't try to get everyone's money but instead target a particular group. This is well demonstrated by restaurants. There are many kinds of food offered, from Italian to Mexican to steakhouses to vegetarian cafés, but there are also differences in the atmosphere (family-friendly or trendy) and price (cheap to fine dining). No restaurant can do it all, and in fact we might actually be wary if we saw a restaurant advertise itself as the best Thai-Hamburger-Ethiopian-Vegan-Fine-Dining-Coffee-Waffle House in the city!

Finding the right group of customers to sell to is called finding a **niche**. The term is taken from biology, where a niche is an environment or ecosystem where a species thrives, like seagulls on a coast or rattlesnakes in a desert. An economic niche is similar; it's that part of the general population of potential buyers (a *segment*) wherein a product will sell well and thus the consumers to whom a seller should pitch his or her goods. A seller who tries to sell comfortable reclining chairs to rambunctious six-year-olds will waste her money courting the wrong segment niche and probably be out of business in no time (unless she switches and targets their tired parents.) A seller, therefore, must have an understanding of population demographics.

In the end, a seller is on a quest, seeking the right segment of buyers who will offer their cups to receive the seller's offering. King Arthur and his knights were also on a quest, to find the Holy Grail, and while theirs was a nobler and less commercial cup search, the parallel provides an easy way to remember five different ways sellers identify the right niche to target, in that sellers seek their products' segment **GRAIL**:

G—gender
R—race or ethnicity
A—age or period in life (such as teens)
I—income level (economy, mid-level, or high-end)
L—lifestyle (sporty, trendy, living in a snowy place, etc.)

***See* Lesson 5A—Seeking the Holy GRAIL**

A couple of things are important to note here in identifying a product's GRAIL.

First, not all of these demographic segments are of concern to every product. Toothbrushes are fine for teeth belonging to a person of any race or gender, though some consider age when buying for children.

Second, some of the perceived differences for segment targeting are more from **social construct** than from scientific evidence of who benefits. Yogurt is of the same nutritional value to men and women yet has been traditionally marketed (pitched) more to women. Many of these social constructs are changing, such as toys now being equally marketed to boys and girls. That may not stop some marketers from trying to convince consumers a product is specially made for them (and thus the consumer should pay more attention, if not dollars).

Another caution to remember is that segment niches categorize people in very general ways. Not all elderly people want to sit at home, nor do all teens want to party all night or follow the latest trend. We must remember that just because someone is part of a segment doesn't mean he or she has to think like everyone in that segment. To assume everyone in a particular segment is the same can be a marketing, and more so a social, error called **stereotyping**. Even trying to formulate such a general idea about a segment may be hazardous, as one must make sure the data the researcher bases his generalizations on are accurate. Judging what all teens like by the tastes of one sixteen-year-old will most likely yield bad data and a **hasty generalization fallacy**, as the **sample size** is not big enough or representative of the group at large.

***See* Lesson 5B—Sample Size Me!**

As consumers, we think of niche targeting (if we do at all) as producers passively watching people and collecting data, following some vague prime directive not to interfere with the indigenous population. It is important to remember, however, at least from a media lit standpoint, that the flow of information goes both ways.

If a little girl never sees another girl in an ad for toy cars, she may get the message that toy cars are not for her and that she should not want to play with them. Similarly, if a boy prefers art to sports, but only sees ads depicting boys playing sports, he might come to believe his preference for art is wrong and he should play sports whether he likes it or not.

In the end, it is important that students know how they are being categorized and then reflect on how much they wish to accept that categorization, so that the **feedback loop** stops, or rather, so that children can step off the merry-go-round of demographic stereotyping if they wish. The more consumers know about themselves and accept however they wish to self-categorize, the less they can be manipulated and compelled to consume products they really don't want or information that is false. The GRAIL challenges all consumers to see themselves from the outside in, asking, "What do marketers assume about me and how much of it is true?"

Many of the five categories of the GRAIL are investigated more deeply in later chapters, especially as to age, but below is a quick overview along with some immediate issues regarding each.

GENDER

Sociologists and psychologists still debate how much gender differences (boys versus girls) are based on inherent biology or society, but we can all agree that much of the messaging communicates that some products and activities are particularly more suitable for one gender over the other. Messaging, as discussed previously, can be overt or, more likely, implied through things like the genders depicted in ads, the description of qualities of either the product or its consumer (tough or dainty), and even the colors (pink or blue) and music (thrashing guitar or light lilt) used in the ad.

The underlying questions such as "Where do our divisions in gender appeal come from?" or "How does/should the gender differentiation change?" are more suited to a psychology or sociology textbook than one on economics and media literacy, but no matter where one's opinion falls in whether gender preferences for certain goods are from biology or society, every individual should be able to choose whether to consume a good and should not be made to feel bad because he doesn't like what is traditionally favored by his gender or because she prefers a product or activity traditionally pitched to others.

See Lesson 5C—Gender Sender

See Lesson 5D—Female Persuasion

RACE

Most products are not targeted to a specific race or ethnicity. Still, marketers will highlight a particular race or ethnicity as a way of saying that their product is specially made with them in mind. It can be a general product, such as fast food, but with a special message to a group, or it can be a product made for the special needs of a member of a race or ethnicity (such as a hair care product).

See Lesson 5E—Seeing Race

In terms of race, America is in a transitional time. The United States historically has been majority white, and as such most media has been geared to white audiences, even if done by unintentionally using that perspective as the default mode for everyone. People of color were often cast, if they were represented at all, in supporting roles to a story about white people, even in ads.

With changing demographics, marketing and media have begun to recognize that everyone responds more positively when they see themselves in media, and to that end ads have begun to have more stories and pitches from non-white perspectives. In the end, this is not just a benefit to the people who see themselves in these new, more inclusive ad pitches, but to everyone who can now see situations from different perspectives, appreciating what we have in common and what is different but, together, contributing to American consumer society.

See Lesson 5F—Sidekicks

AGE

Age is the most mutable, or changing, of the five aspects of the GRAIL. This can create a dilemma for marketers; once their brand is preferred by customers of a certain age group, say *tweens* (ten- to twelve-year-olds), is it better for the seller to "grow up" with their customers and then offer teen-oriented products or to stay in their age niche and try to win over a new generation of customers? The marketer might think that they've already done the hard part of winning over a population, but then again, how much does that population associate the brand with their younger, former selves, an age and time they would now prefer to leave behind to be more grown-up? On the other hand, a marketer might take the same product and give it a varied appeal simply by presenting the product with a pitch suitable for each age group targeted.

See **Lesson 5G—Jus4U**

One other special note about age is how often young people do not buy for the age group they are, but for the age group they wish to be (**aspirational buying**). Tweens will look to teens for consumption inspiration, while teens might look at young adults in an attempt to be like sophisticated twenty-somethings. For marketers, this might lead them to pitch to a consumer, not where they are in terms of emotional or psychological development, but prematurely to where the consumer wants to be.

Can this be a problem? Some say it leads to **KGOY**, or **Kids Getting Older Younger**, wherein younger consumers might rush to buy a product that they do not fully understand (such as a tween T-shirt that says, "Sexy!") or even eventually be led to or exposed to situations they are not ready to handle, be it watching it in media or partaking of it in real life. It also creates the possibility that young people will get a poor idea of future phases in life. As with fantasy, ads make for poor survey samplings of reality. Then again, even many adults are vulnerable to age-related fantasy messages, especially messages that say consumption of a product makes the adult young again!

INCOME

In the United States, people are taught that it is rude to inquire about or discuss income levels (one might note that in other countries, asking how much another person earns at their job is showing polite curiosity and interest). In fact, America prides itself on having a historically fluid class structure, creating the ideal of "rags to riches" opportunity.

As such, the norm is that differing income segments are often not overtly addressed but are appealed to by way of implicit language that then becomes understood by the audience (in politics, such indirect messaging has been labeled as **dog whistles**, implying that only certain segments can hear or be attuned to the call or real message). No one would ever say that their product is "for the rich," but they might say it is "high-end" or a "luxury" product (such as "gourmet" for food) and include visuals of affluent people using the product. At the other end of the economic scale, words like "budget" or "economy" might be used, again along with visuals to suit.

See Lesson 5H—Income in Code

Similar to what we see regarding the Age category, many consumers buy not for where they are income-wise, but where they aspire to be someday. This can be seen in consumers buying more in terms of quality or quantity than they need, and while this is a personal decision, the risk is that such a vulnerable consumer might be "nudged" into unwise or ill-informed choices, especially as to lack of savings and debt accumulation.

The original theory of a **free-market society** was that a consumer, looking at a product, would decide for herself whether a demanded price was fair considering the quality and utility of the product. This might have been true back when people purchased few goods, most often from trusted people they knew in the community, but today's consumer is asked to consider claims about many products, from the wet-road grip of tires, to the speed of computers, to the health benefits of acai berries or quinoa, that they may not be in a position to adequately evaluate, and they may not know the salesperson well enough to trust his or her claims. So what do we consumers do?

Often, people will opt not to buy the cheapest or the most expensive but settle on the middle-priced good, assuming its quality is not too much or too little. Whereas Goldilocks tested her options before she chose, this blind middle choice system turns the free-market system on its head as we no longer judge if a price is fair based on the quality of the product, but instead judge the quality of the product based on the price! As we will see later on, with a little pre-research on the part of the buyer, we can restore the transactional balance (and the Force) in the universe!

See Lesson 5I—Price Is Right?

LIFESTYLE

Lifestyle is the broadest of the categories, as it covers all the different ways we live our lives. It's also the category in which we get to have the most choice and power. A sixteen-year-old may be part of a single gender, race, age, and income segment, but she might be a part of one lifestyle on weekdays (student), another in the late afternoons (athlete), and a third on the weekends (a hobby such as surfing or collecting). It's not just what we do that determines lifestyle but also what communities we identify and associate with, whether based on religious beliefs, geography, or sexuality. In fact, there are so many facets to lifestyle, every person is probably a unique combination of all different lifestyles and accompanying degrees of participation and enjoyment of each.

Despite all the permutations and subcategories a single person's lifestyle provides, people often prefer simple labels, so we tend to put people in groups (even while we ourselves resist being put in a one-dimensional category). Perhaps it is acceptable to put people in general categories for certain activities (shopping for what they might like for a present), but we should never let such presumptions cloud us from seeing the total person.

See **Lesson 5J—Lifestyle Personal Shopper**

CHAPTER 5 ACCOMPANYING LESSONS

Lesson 5A—Seeking the Holy GRAIL

Key Concepts

understanding consumer demographics, **niche** and **niche targeting**, **GRAIL**

Special Materials/Media

Ad Analysis Sheet, plus magazines, TV, or other commercial media

Intro Questions/Thoughts for Students

- Are most products/stores made for everybody, or are they tailored to particular groups (*segments*)? What are the different groups, and how do sellers make their product and advertisements (**pitches**) appeal to different groups?

Activity

Create and distribute an Ad Analysis Sheet (see sample below) to determine the segment of society that a product and its advertising is targeting. Some categories may not matter for a particular ad (it may sell to both men and women, for example), but have students try to figure out where the ad focuses in on a particular group.

Alternatively, the teacher can also:

- Divide the class into pre-assigned GRAIL groups to look for ads fitting their group.
- Have a scavenger hunt for finding as many different GRAIL combinations as possible.

Follow-up Questions/Discussions

- Do some kinds of products specialize in one group more than others? Why do most sellers target a specific group? Why not try to appeal to everyone?
- Why do some things get labeled as only for a particular group? For example, some exercise equipment, such as pink stretch bands marketed for

women, is equally usable by men. Or tools predominantly advertised to men?

- As a follow-up have students look at a store or brand that appeals to their parents but not to them and point out the GRAIL distinctions (see Ad Analysis Sheet) between the appeal to parents and themselves. Do so again for a brand or store that appeals to the student but not their parents.

Social Questions for Students

- Have you ever tried to make everyone happy, even for a small group? What strategy for compromise do you have when not everyone likes the same thing or can't get what they want?
- How can you try to understand why someone likes something that doesn't appeal to you?

Ad Analysis Sheet (Sample)

Brand and product advertised:

____

Medium of ad (magazine, TV, radio, billboard):

____

Location of ad (time and place seen on TV, URL, name of magazine, etc.):

____

The Holy GRAIL (five segment niches):

Gender target:

____

Race (or ethnicity) target:

____

Age group target:

____

Income level (low, middle, high) target:

____

Lifestyle (such as sporty, business professional, rebel, retired, etc.) target:

____

____

Technique/style used to appeal to that *segment niche* (what is being done to make it appeal to that particular group?):

____

____

Lesson 5B—Sample Size Me!

Key Concepts

consumer demographics, **GRAIL**, social science survey methodology, **sample sizes** and data collection

Special Materials/Media

None

Intro Questions/Thoughts for Students

- We all hear of popular or hit TV shows, songs, and other media that "everyone" seems to be enjoying, but are there differences and can we discover trends among the population as to what is popular?

Activity

Have students put together a two-part survey such as this:

1. *What is your current favorite...*

Movie	TV show	Music artist	[something else, such as restaurant or place to hang out]

2. *If you would not mind saying, what is your...*

Gender	Race	Age	Family Income (high, middle, low)	Lifestyle (what are you into/being?)

Students may modify questions, but as to the GRAIL questions, it is important that surveyors follow guidelines:

1. People surveyed (respondents) should answer for themselves (how they *self-perceive*). The questioner should not answer for them.
2. "I don't know" or "I don't want to say" should be accepted responses without questioning (enter *IDK* for "I don't know" or *RNS* for "Rather not say").

3. If respondents ask for clarification, the surveyors should have some agreed examples. For example, if a respondent asks, "What do you mean by *Lifestyle*?" the class could agree to say, "It means what activities do you do that you think define who you are, like athlete, church-goer, home-body, etc."

Students should survey as many people as possible and then aggregate the data and compare the responses five ways (by each GRAIL category) to look for trends.

Follow-up Questions/Discussions

- Did any trends stick out? Were the trends more prominent (greater) by one GRAIL category than another?
- Did you get an even number of respondents from each GRAIL category? Did you get enough from each category for a fair representation (**sample size**)? For which categories might you want to get more responses?
- You can compare your survey top choices with national ones by looking at sites like Nielsen (http://www.nielsen.com/us/en/top10s.html). If your responses did not match the national favorites, why do you think that is?
- Why do you think it was important to let people self-identify their categories rather than the questioner deciding? What are the advantages and disadvantages of doing it that way?
- Why is it important that the questioners have a consistent way of doing the survey (*methodology*)? How might inconsistent methods change the data collected?
- When we say a show, movie, or song is "hot" or popular, are we getting the whole picture? Is there a difference between the category leader being the majority pick (chosen by over 50 percent of the respondents) and being the plurality pick (most common choice but under 50 percent)?

Social Questions for Students

- Have you ever felt pressure to like something just because everyone else likes it? When is it OK to just "go along" and when should you speak up (and maybe opt out)?
- Do you ever feel bad because you don't like what everyone around you likes? Do you think about people differently because they like or dislike something else?

Lesson 5C—Gender Sender

Key Concepts
preconceptions based on gender
Special Materials/Media
picture of a horse or other animal
Intro Questions/Thoughts for Students

- When we look at something new, do we start with preconceived ideas? How much are we assessing something neutrally versus imposing our already formed ideas onto a situation or thing?

Picture of horse (ambiguous gender). Joachim Marian Winkler, "Horse," Pixabay, https://pixabay.com/en/arabs-stallion-thoroughbred-arabian-1367173/.

Activity

Students should show the picture to people outside of the class and explain, "This is a picture of a male/female horse. Please look at it and tell me three adjectives you would use to describe it." Half of the student surveyors should say *male*; half should say *female*; but everyone uses the *same* picture. Questioners should try not to overemphasize the words *male/female* so as not to give away the variable being tested. Student surveyors should also note the gender of the respondent.

The class should then tabulate the results and assemble lists of the most common adjectives used to describe the perceived male horse and the perceived female horse. If possible, break down the responses by the respondents' gender to see if there is a difference.

Follow-up Questions/Discussions

- Was there a significant difference in the adjectives used? If there were differences, did the different adjectives correspond to adjectives traditionally given to males (strong, bold) and females (graceful, beautiful)?
- Was there a difference between male and female respondents? Was one group more equal in their adjectives? If so, why do you think that is?
- This is a modification of a 2002 experiment done where Spanish and German subjects were shown a picture of a bridge. (In Spanish, bridge, *el puente*, is male and in German, *die brucke*, it is female.) The adjectives used by subjects to describe the bridge corresponded to traditional male/female adjectives, such as *beautiful*, *elegant*, *fragile*, and *pretty* for those who saw the bridge as female and *dangerous*, *strong*, *sturdy*, and *towering* for those who saw the bridge as male. What conclusions do you make based on that experiment? We do not have male/female articles in English, but do we still impose ideas based on whether we perceive the object as male/female?

Social Questions for Students

- Do we superimpose our expectations and judgments on people? Do we assume they are supposed to be one way or the other? When is that OK and when is it not?
- On the receiving end, how do you feel when people assume you must be good or bad at something because of your gender (or another attribute)? Is there a difference if they assume something good or something bad about you?

Lesson 5D—Female Persuasion

Key Concepts
gender roles and media
Special Materials/Media
videos or Internet
Intro Questions/Thoughts for Students

- When we watch a movie or read a story, we focus mainly on the plot and whether we are entertained, but are there also messages being sent to girls and boys about how they should behave? If enough small messages are sent, can it add up (the **stalagmite effect**)?
- Can you think of any rules that apply only to boys or girls? Why do we have those rules?
- Can you think of anything that "boys can get away with" or that "girls can get away with" that the other can't?

Activity

When it comes to a woman controlling her own destiny, we could put *Cinderella* at one end of a spectrum (passive heroine taken care of by her godmother until ultimately living happily ever after by being taken care of by a prince) and *Mulan* or *Wonder Woman* at the other (active heroine who defies tradition and society to save the country/world). Given this passive to active spectrum, where are other cartoon women that girls watch and see as role models?

Have students compile lists and rewatch children's shows to take note of the messages about women, and then create a "power line" or continuum and place characters along it after discussing where each should go.

- How many of the heroines are active versus passive changers of the world? Compare that to the female villains. Who are more assertive, the female heroes or the female villains?
- When the females are taking action, is it to address major issue and as the lead, or to a side issue and as the support to someone else?
- How much does the female take the lead in a romance? Does the boy more often pursue the girl, the girl the boy, or is it about even?
- When characters fall for another character, is it based on their object of desire's looks, talents (such as the sound of their voice), or personality (such as kindness)?
- How much does shopping/consumerism play a part in girls' vs. boys' lives in film?

- In the end ("happily ever after"), does the woman join the man's life (such as Ariel leaving her family and environment), the man join the woman's, or are they equal?

Follow-up Questions/Discussions

- What are the messages given to girls? Often in movies, the girl signifies her new self (new inside) by a new look outside (which is usually prettier or at least with more make-up, such as in *Grease*!). While the girl often comes to realize it's what's on the inside that counts, does she then save time and effort by going back to her old look? Does this send a mixed message then about looks? Do boy heroes have the same message?
- What other sources send messages about active/passive nature to girls? Ads? News stories?
- How do you think boys are affected by these messages to girls? What do they think of "aggressive women" or girls who don't worry so much about how they look to others?
- What do you think of the "It's just a movie" counter-argument? Do you agree that such media have limited (if at all) effects?

Social Questions for Students

- Do you think the message about active/passive female roles is changing with your generation? Have the heroines changed over time? How so? When a heroine is strong, is her strength accepted as natural or spotlighted as unusual? As a follow-up, interview a parent as to his or her impression of a movie and its message.
- Is it OK for someone to say they just want life to take care of them, that they are happy to just ride out whatever wave carries them through life? If your best friend said that their dream was to look good so that they can find someone who will marry and take care of them, what would you say?

Lesson 5E—Seeing Race

Key Concepts
GRAIL, race in media
Special Materials/Media
Access to photo
Intro Questions/Thoughts for Students

- Do we see things without even noticing we are seeing them?

- When it comes to demographic differences, you often hear people say, "I don't see race/color." What does that mean? Does it mean they don't see it or it doesn't matter to them?
- If we see something only subconsciously, how can that affect us in making decisions?

Activity

Students should find a picture with lots of random objects in it plus people of different races (better if they create such a picture in their classroom). Students then become surveyors who tell respondents that this will be a memory test: the respondent is to look at the picture for thirty seconds and then will be asked questions. Students should make a list of five questions such as "What color was the wall?" but also include "How many people of color (non-white) were in the picture?" Students then tabulate the results.

Follow-up Questions/Discussions

- Based on your experiment, would you conclude people see differences in race even if they aren't directed to look for it?
- How does the overall accuracy in identifying the number of people of color compare to the accuracy for other responses? What do you interpret from that?
- Why is it important not to reveal right away that this is an experiment about race?

Social Questions for Students

- How often do you "see" things about someone without being aware that you are seeing them? Does it depend whether you are focused on the person or in a crowded room? Can seeing such things subconsciously affect how you treat them?
- Is it rude to ask someone about her race or ethnicity out of curiosity? What is the best way to do so? Even if your question is politely phrased, why might it bother her?

Lesson 5F—Sidekicks

Key Concepts
   GRAIL, race in media
Special Materials/Media
   Access to TV shows or movies
Intro Questions/Thoughts for Students

- We are seeing more people of color in media (TV shows and movies), but how are such characters being incorporated? Are characters of color the main focus or sidekicks who lend assistance to main, white characters or who just add a "difference" to a show?

Activity

Students watch their favorite shows or movies. As they watch, they should try to look for and take note of characters of color. As they do so, they should take notes and reflect on the portrayal:

- How many of the characters of color are the main focus of the plot?
- Do you know a lot about the characters or just one facet (like they run a certain store)?
- Do the characters of color do something that is stereotypical of that race/ethnicity (like play rap music)?
- What kind of "power" do the characters of color have? Intellectual, physical, magical? Are they using their power to help themselves or the main character?

Follow-up Questions/Discussions

- Did you find more main characters to be white characters with sidekicks of color or main characters of color with white sidekicks?
- When you found a central character who was a person of color, was he or she the only one or part of a group? What was the apparent racial balance of the group?
- Why do you think central characters are predominantly white? As of 2017, non-Hispanic whites constitute about 60 percent of the population; does that correspond with the rough percentage you found represented?
- Could your class's numbers be affected by the kinds of shows you all watched, which in turn might be affected by the races of the people doing the observations? This could be a **sampling error**. What can you do to correct that?
- There are many movies and shows with central characters that are predominantly non-white, but often such media have lower ratings for white audiences. Why do you think that may be?
- Do you think your findings might be different in cultures that consisted primarily of what we in the United States call people of color, such as in Asia, Africa, or Latin America? Do they have, for example, a single white character as a funny, comic sidekick? How can you find out?

Social Questions for Students

- Have you ever been part of a group but still felt "outnumbered" or somehow "apart"? What did you do?
- How can we make sure everyone is included as equally as they want to be without calling obvious or even embarrassing attention to the situation?
- How do we "share power" socially, so that everyone who wants to can have a chance to lead?

Lesson 5G—Jus4U

Key Concepts
segment niche, specialization of product regarding age
Special Materials/Media
None (camera if you wish to have students film outside of class)
Intro Questions/Thoughts for Students

- How would you change a product's attributes or the messaging (sales pitch) depending on the age of the customer?

Activity

For a product or service, like shampoo or a restaurant, have groups design and act out TV ads (each thirty seconds to one minute) five ways:

- ad designed to sell to children
- ad designed to sell to tweens (ages nine to twelve)
- ad designed to sell to teens
- ad designed to sell to parents (midthirties)
- ad designed to sell to senior citizens

This can be done in class with prep time or as an improv challenge (with three to four minutes between to change the ad).

In making the ads appeal to the different age groups, consider both:

- *content* (the part of the experience emphasized) and
- *format* (pace, tone, language, camera angles, and action).

Follow-up Questions/Discussions

- What were the differences in the product attributes? Why do they differ?

- What were the differences in the sales pitches? Why do they differ? Did students think about what appealed to their audience? How did they figure out what appealed to them?
- With only thirty seconds to demonstrate your ad, did you have to generalize about the tastes and appeals of the target age groups? What kind of message might it send to people watching it?
- Do they see this in real advertising? In what way? There is an international award for best ads, the *Clio* (https://clios.com/). Take a look at the best ads of the past years. Why do you think they are considered the best? Do you agree?
- Why do some places, including social netowrks, have minimum ages?

Social Questions for Students

- Why do we like different things (or no longer like some things) as we get older?
- Do you like the same things you liked five years ago? Is it OK to still like some of those things (TV shows, fashion, toys)?
- What does it mean to "grow up" in terms of preferences? What do you like now that you think you will not like in five years?
- Is it OK to change who we like (or don't) in our circle of friends as we get older?
- Is it OK for a company (such as Starbucks) to limit their customers to a certain age group? For example, if late twenty-somethings spend a lot of money and don't like teens hanging in their favorite coffee shop, can the store keep the teens out? What about other aspects (gender, race, etc.)?
- Are there dangers to ingnoring minimum age requirements, from brick-and-mortar places to social networks?

Lesson 5H—Income in Code

Key Concepts

segment niche, specialization of product regarding income

Special Materials/Media

Access to advertising

Intro Questions/Thoughts for Students

- As Americans, we consider it rude to openly discuss money, including price or affordability, sometimes. Instead, we use adjectives such as "luxury," "affordable," or "economy" to indicate how much something costs or to what economic level it is being advertised. Even when ads do say a price (such as automobile ads), such words are still used for reinforcement.

- What other words are used to imply socioeconomic targets of an ad?

Activity

Have students watch ads for products aimed at low-, moderate-, and high-income buyers, either as judged by the product itself or the store. They should try to come up with a list of code words used to imply the economic level. Look also at the people, setting, music, and other common factors in making such ads.

Now, put into groups, the students have been hired by a restaurant, *Chez Füd*, that sells many kinds of food (so the students can choose which to emphasize). They are to make three ads targeting each economic group without mentioning price but just using the cues like they saw from watching ads.

For their ads, they must fill out a plan sheet first that indicates:

- word cues
- actor cues
- time, place, or manner of ad cues

As the others in the class watch the ads, they must take note of how many of the planned cues they can see.

Follow-up Questions/Discussions

- Which of the three was the easiest to make? Which was the hardest? Why?
- Did you use any stereotypes about people of a certain income? Were they positive or negative? Were they fair? If someone of that economic group watched your ad, would they be persuaded or insulted?
- If there is a negative tone to one ad, why so? Why isn't there a negative tone to the others?

Social Questions for Students

- It is socially unacceptable to make fun of someone because of their gender or race. Do you feel it is equally unacceptable to think less of someone or even make fun of them because of their family's income level? Why do kids who come from lower economic families sometimes feel embarrassed that they cannot afford some things (given they have as little control of their circumstances as someone born to an affluent family)?
- Do you think other countries attach similar social standing and value to wealth versus poverty?

- Have you ever been embarrassed to tell someone you can't afford to do something? What would you think if a friend told you he could not afford to do an activity you really wanted to do together?

Lesson 5I—Price Is Right?

Key Concepts

judging quality by price rather than price by quality, statistical significance

Special Materials/Media

three kinds of cookies

Intro Questions/Thoughts for Students

- As buyers, we are supposed to have **sovereignty**, which means we get to decide if a product is worth the price, but do we sometimes let the price tell us what is good quality?
- If you go to the store and have to buy something you don't know anything about, would you buy the most expensive, least expensive, or middle-priced one? Why?

Activity

The class should set up a taste test for cookies (or a test station for nail polish or some other product). Explain to test subjects that they are needed to help decide which cookies the class will sell or have at a party. The three samples are labeled A, B, and C but should be introduced as "This is our basic," "This is our middle one," and "This is our ultra." Ask the people to rank the three. What the tasters do not know is that the cookies are from the same batch (or from comparable ones). Tabulate preference results.

Follow-up Questions/Discussions

- Did people prefer the high end more or all equally?
- Is the difference statistically significant (generally more than 5 percent difference), to rule out chance?
- An important part of being a social scientist is acting or not giving away what you are testing (otherwise people might change their answer). Were some testers better than others at not giving it away? How can you make everyone better so the data isn't "tainted"?
- What do you think would happen if you gave out expensive cookies as "low end" and cheaper ones as "high end"? Would people be able to tell?

- Instead of adjectives, what if you called the cookies by name brands known for low end, middle, and high end? Do you think that would affect people?

Social Questions for Students

- How often do we convince ourselves of preferring something or someone because we are "supposed" to like it/them more? Is that wrong? How can we better check ourselves to make sure we truly like something and not just because we are supposed to?
- Is there anything wrong with admiring or liking something because it is worth more money or costs more? What are the potential downsides of valuing things by how much they cost?
- Some people say they feel better about themselves when they "treat themselves" to expensive things. Is this OK? Do you feel better about yourself when you spend more money on yourself or someone spends a lot of money on a gift to you?
- How do you feel about people who try not to spend a lot? Do you think less about them?
- For all of the questions above, substitute "time" for the idea of "money"; are your answers the same?

Lesson 5J—Lifestyle Personal Shopper

Key Concepts
segment niche, specialization of product regarding lifestyle
Special Materials/Media
Visit to a mall or online shopping
Intro Questions/Thoughts for Students

- While we tend to think of people in general groups (musicians, athletes, superheroes, friends) and thus similar to one another, there can be differences in personal tastes. How much do the tastes for a certain category of people overlap while still being different?

Activity

The class should think of a category of fictional characters (teens, wizards, superheroes, etc.). For that category, make a list of members, and then tell pairs or groups of three that they are in charge of pretend shopping for a gift but at real stores. For a randomly assigned character in that category the group must find:

- one gift related to the character being a member of that category and
- one gift that is uniquely personal to that character's way of life.

They have a *total* budget of $100. Each group must make a presentation of what they would have bought and why.

Follow-up Questions/Discussions

- Was it harder to buy the category gift or the personal gift?
- Between the groups, was there more similarity between the category gifts or the personal gifts?
- How do the gifts show the characters are similar and different?
- Did you find things at one particular store, with one brand, or in many places? Which real-life store would be your character's favorite?
- If you were doing this for nonfictional characters (such as your teachers), do different stores/brands cater to their different lifestyles?

Social Questions for Students

- Are there assumptions you make about a person because he wears or uses a certain brand?
- Do you feel better about yourself or your "look" when you wear a particular brand? Why?
- Do you feel better about yourself when you wear what most of your friends are wearing or when you have on something very different that makes you stand out?
- To be part of a group, how much should a person be willing to conform?

Chapter Six

An Age-Old Question

If you have any recollection of your middle-school days, or have ever taught math, then chances are you know why six is afraid of seven . . . because seven **ate** nine! If this is new to you, we can pause while you consider the philosophical and social implications of cannibal numbers, but for the rest, why is that joke no longer funny? Most will tell you that the joke got old, but like a man in an Einstein problem watching a clock on a train moving at the speed of light, it's relative; it's less that the joke got old as *we* did!

As we explored last chapter, we consumers can be segmented in five ways, collectively called the GRAIL. Each has their own special issues, but the age category is special because it's the one guaranteed to change. Biologists may roll their eyes at the idea that our cells regenerate every seven years and thus we are "new people," but the fact is that biological maturation and change, combined with life experiences over time, create a new "you," at least in world perspective. The ancient Greek philosopher Heraclitus stated that one can never step in the same river twice because the river constantly changes, but it's also in many ways a new you doing the stepping out.

We'll leave further philosophy to our toga-clad colleagues, but for our purposes, the concept of perpetual change deserves special attention because the world's messages to people, and how people in turn process those messages, change with age. Whether it's a product (what is a "good" car) or a message (who are "good" people), we process it differently at six than at sixteen, twenty-six, or eighty-six.

See **Lesson 6A—Age-jectives**

THE CENTRICS

A popular ad once asked, "What would you do for a Klondike bar?" Before that, a spokesperson said he'd "walk a mile for a Camel [cigarette]" (even if continued use of said Camels reduced his ability to walk said mile). What these two ads, and many others, touch upon is that we all have weaknesses; there are some things folks just have to have and would do just about anything to get.

While such ads acknowledge physical cravings, what they insidiously don't mention is that they are simultaneously playing on consumers' invisible, but just as strong, emotional needs. Abraham Maslow famously published what he perceived as the *hierarchy of people's needs* in his 1943 paper "A Theory of Human Motivation." It would take a whole other book to explain Maslow's hierarchy in detail, but his theory is that all human beings have a similar pyramid of needs:

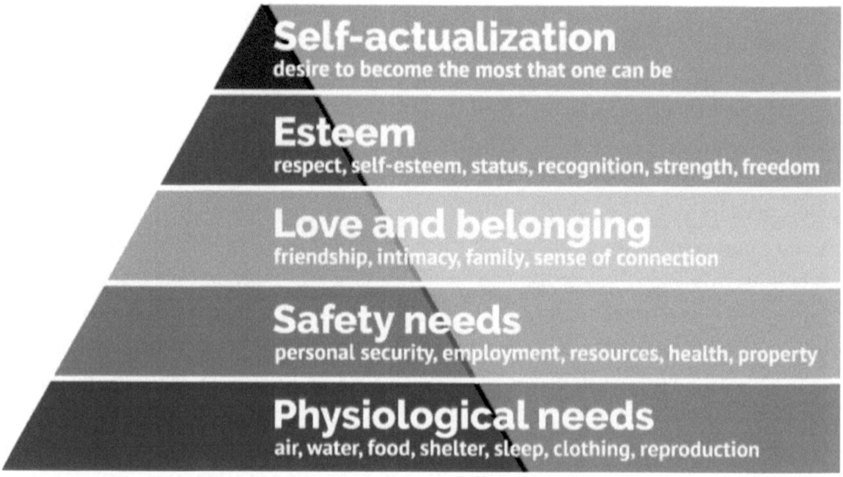

Maslow's hierarchy of needs pyramid. Saul McLeod, "Maslow's Hierarchy of Needs," Simply Psychology, https://www.simplypsychology.org/maslow.html.

As Maslow describes it, the higher, more cognitive and emotional needs rest on a basis of physiological and practical needs, but in general we can say that the lower, base needs make living achievable, while the higher needs make life worthwhile. The media persuaders, whether in ads for cars or in campaign speeches, often format their appeals to say that our needs will be met by consumption of their product or agreement with their ideas.

Each of us is a unique combination of GRAIL categories, yet we all need a "sense of belonging," even if that sense varies from person to person. One person's idea of "belonging" may be thinking of cuddling with a life partner, while another may think of hanging out with a peer group, while still another may think of a team project achieving some never-before-realized breakthrough (such as a device that keeps a cat from waking up people at 4:00 a.m. because it's hungry or lonely or just because it's a cat).

Still, research has found that there are some more detailed commonalities and that these commonalities can generally be leveled by age group. These common needs by age have been variously named, but here we shall call them **centrics**,[1] or the emotional and psychological needs of a particular age group. They are the sunshine that the plant grows toward, even if the direction from which the sunlight comes changes. A tween's incontrovertibly cool T-shirt is yesterday's embarrassment once she is a teen, and perhaps a nostalgic remembrance once she is an adult.

Much of the work in identifying youth centrics was done and continues to be done by child, developmental, and adolescent psychologists. It is noteworthy, however, that leaning over the shoulders of these researchers (who do it to help children) are marketers and purveyors of information, looking for the perfect appeal to a centric that will make their message be gladly ingested. This is why teachers need to help students realize what those centrics are at a given stage, not so that students will refuse to satisfy those centric-driven cravings, but to make healthier choices in satisfying them. We all crave sweets, but good nutrition information might make us reach for sweet fruit rather than candy, and we'll all live better for it.

Children's Centrics

The authors of this book are Texans. That might not seem important to you, but it is in this context.[2] An important rule for Texans is to never cut to the chase when a story can first be told (that we tell stories mainly about dead people is what qualified us to be classified as history teachers).

So, way back at the turn of the millennium, one of us was watching a certain kid's cable channel (we won't mouse around and tell you which one, even if you are all ears) with his six-year-old son (whom we will call "Ben" to avoid family embarrassment). Ben loved this channel, including a show called *Movie Surfers*, in which kids seemingly reviewed movies that were almost always made by the movie production arm (or other ear) of this corporate conglomerate.

On this particular episode, the kid-reviewers were discussing a movie just released that, frankly, had horrible reviews, with one reviewer saying he wanted to know from whom to demand the ninety minutes of his life back. Nevertheless, the kids on the show *loved* the movie and raved about it excitedly. Ben, not wanting to miss out on this childhood phantasm of fun, turned and said, "Dad, we've *got* to go see it!"

Dad, being the wise economics teacher who wanted his child to understand that these supposedly earnest children were shills for a corporation bent on taking his future college funds, asked, "Ben, why do you think these kids are telling the truth?" Ben thought for a moment and then teared up in world-crashing panic as he said, "But why would other kids not tell the truth? Are they *lying* to me?"

An important lesson was learned that day . . . by the dad: to never introduce thoughtful but undermining questions about a child's favorite show, or at least to not pull back the curtain revealing the man behind it too soon (and further to immediately minimize family angst by taking Ben to see said movie, for which Ben gave it a grade of thoroughly "meh"). On the other hand, the story also illustrates that children should not be thought of as just future players in a marketers-versus-media lit game of the future; they are playing the game *now* and they are playing against professionals without even knowing it.

Meanwhile, back in Texas, we are aware that some think of our education system as something we do to kill time between weekend football, but many breakthroughs have come out of our universities. One professor, however, is very controversial in his breakthroughs regarding children and media.

In 1992, James McNeal, a marketing professor at Texas A&M, published a seminal book, *Kids as Customers*,[3] which laid out how marketing and messaging can be effectively used in regard to the under-ten set. Many marketers grabbed up a copy and still see it as a how-to guide to persuade children. Media lit people, on the other hand, see it as an insight into the other team's playbook, and herein it will be used to devise counter-defenses (see, as Texans, we couldn't stay away from football that long!).

McNeal considered children to be part of three markets: as current customers, as influencers on their parents' decisions (sometimes called "the nag factor"), and as future consumers who will hopefully have a lot more buying power once they are adults with tastes influenced from childhood. Thus, according to McNeal, winning the child market can yield up to three returns on an investment.

Beyond pure marketing of products, McNeal's observations lead to two further insights in the field of media lit. First, whatever McNeal said about kids as consumers of tangible goods, including the three-markets-in-one, also applies to children as receivers of ideas and value messages. Second, as children are already desired and sought after by marketers, it is necessary they be educated in media literacy as early as possible so as to be discriminating consumers of products and information (never forgetting that parents remain the gatekeepers as much as possible).

Sellers will call it **market penetration**, or merely informing potential consumers of choices, but when looked at from a media lit point of view, it could also be called colonizing our children and our future. Or, if you want it straight from the marketers' mouths, consider the following quotes as reported by Gary Ruskin in his 2003 article, "Why They Whine: How Corporations Prey on Our Children":[4]

- "Children should be viewed as economic resources to be mined."
- "Children are the brightest star in the consumer constellation."
- "If you own this child at an early age, you can own this child for years to come."
- "If you tell [children] to buy something, they are resistant. But if you tell them that they'll be a dork if they don't, you've got their attention. You open up emotional vulnerabilities, and it's very easy to do with kids because they're the most emotionally vulnerable."

See Lesson 6B—About Face

See Lesson 6C—Drawing a Conclusion

Regarding the centrics, or points of appeal, American children can be said to have three. First, they want the love and approval of their parents, teachers, and friends. To obtain this validation, children often imitate and adopt the identity, views, and behaviors of their immediate group as their own, so that they can feel a member of a protected tribe, as it were. They also may do so because there is simply no other example for them to see, such that theirs is not so much a choice to follow the dominant norm but an acceptance of what they perceive as the sole existent way to act and think. From a marketing and messaging point of view, a child can be encouraged to want a certain product or do a certain activity or espouse a certain view by sending the child the message that doing so will give them that sense of *belonging*.

See Lesson 6D—Fun Me Downs

A second centric for kids is amusement—plain and simple *fun*. Whether learning or relaxing, kids respond better to information if it is presented as engaging and entertaining. Even if the thing itself (such as brushing teeth) is not inherently a top joy of life, turning it into a game or wrapping the event in colors and music (such as musical toothbrushes) will draw kids into whatever message is being promoted. In 2002, a convention centered on Advertising and Promoting to Kids (APK) in New York even featured a session titled "Owning Fun! Reaching Kids through Product Innovation, Package Design and Brand Graphics"; and you thought fun was for everyone to own and share![5]

See Lesson 6E—And We'll Have Fun, Fun, Fun till Daddy Takes the Toy-bird Away

The third centric available for utilization as a delivery tool for messaging children is their desire to be grown up. From an early age, kids want to dress up, be big, and enjoy all the perks of adulthood (until they hear about taxes, mortgages, and how the plumbing always breaks during peak charge hours). So much do kids want to hang with the big boys that they will consume, even gulp down, anything that older, more respected people (often siblings) consume, even if they don't understand it themselves.

This phenomenon is called **aspirational buying** and can be easily exploited to get kids to say things they don't yet comprehend (such as a fake tattoo that says "sexy") or the implications of which they don't realize ("all ____ people are bad"). At the same APK convention mentioned above, the keynote address was titled "Emotional Branding for Kids: Creating Lifelong Consumers." One expects parents would take umbrage at strangers devising how to 'brand' their children.

See Lesson 6F—Older Younger

With all three centrics, it's preferable to say that messages **convey** them rather than *depict* them. *Depict* really just means the author or artist is showing what they are thinking, regardless of whether the viewer or reader gets the message. *Convey*, on the other hand, is to carry something from one point to another, or share one person's idea with another. If the viewer or reader does not get the message of belonging, fun, or aspiration, then the idea was not conveyed and the message was a failure, like passing a basketball that goes out of bounds. In the end, it's not the messages depicted that have an impact; it's the ones that are conveyed.

Why have middle-school kids learn how media influences children (who are generally classified as under ten, or elementary age)? First, many younger middle schoolers, developmentally, are still operating with a child's view of the world, as opposed to a tween (see below) mindset, especially given that different school systems define "middle school" as beginning anywhere from fourth to seventh grade.

Second, having older middle-school students, such as seventh and eighth graders (who are decidedly tweens), examine techniques used for children gives them an "older person" perspective. They can see better the manipulation and folly of youth by looking back, which then allows them to consider their present situation and be more receptive to learning the techniques currently used on tweens like them. If they can see that a brand or idea can envelope a child so much that the child assumes it is the **norm**, excluding competing brands or perspectives, might the tweens now start to see that phenomenon in their own world?

See **Lesson 6G—From PG to G**

See **Lesson 6H—Schooling You in Ads**

CHAPTER 6 ACCOMPANYING LESSONS

Lesson 6A—Age-jectives

Key Concepts
changing perspectives due to age
Special Materials/Media
Access to media
Intro Questions/Thoughts for Students

- How do our perspectives change by age?
- Can you name a product, show, or activity that is generally seen differently by people of different ages? Why do they look at it differently?

Activity

Students should list a wide variety of brands and stores that they know, such as Nike, Old Navy, or Walmart. For each brand or store, students should list three adjectives to describe someone who regularly wears that brand or shops at that store. The answers should then be compared to find the three most common adjectives for each. Also, take a vote whether there is a general positive, negative, or neutral feeling toward the brand or store.

As a next step, students should then ask people of different ages to list their three adjectives for users of the same brands/stores. Students, in asking, should make sure to note the age of the person giving the response (adult, teen, tween [ten to twelve], or below ten).

Students should also ask whether the subject's feelings are generally "positive," "negative," or "neutral" toward the brand or store. All of the results should then be sorted by respondents' ages to determine the three most common adjectives for users of the brands/stores by the age groups, as well as the general feeling toward them.

Follow-up Questions/Discussions

- How much did the adjectives differ? Do you see any commonalities in adjectives despite the age differences? What does that tell you about the brand's or store's reputation or image?
- How often were people completely unfamiliar with a brand or store? Were there any trends (such as older people were less familiar)? What does that tell you about the brand's or store's reputation or targeted consumer?
- What was the trend in general feeling (positive/negative/neutral) toward brands or stores? Any patterns, such as growing more or less positive as older people give their opinion?
- Were any adjectives used both positively *and* negatively (such as "rebellious" or "cheap")? What do you make of that?
- Do you feel any one group's view is "righter" than another's (other than that you agree with that opinion)? Does it depend on whom the brand/store is meant to be for?

Social Questions for Students

- Is there a difference between tolerating something another person likes but you don't (such as music or a fashion trend) and accepting it?
- If an older person tells you something you like is "bad," what should you do? What if it is the other way around, where you think what an older person does is "bad"? What can you do to understand, if not agree, with each other?

Lesson 6B—About Face

Key Concepts

market penetration of children, cultural impression of children

Special Materials/Media

Access to Internet to either put together slideshow (such as with PowerPoint) or to print pictures

Intro Questions/Thoughts for Students

- Who are the most important people in America? Who are the most well-known? What is the difference? How much do they overlap?
- How many professional athletes from your hometown or state can you name? TV or film stars? How about scientists or even Nobel Laureates?
- How many of the above personalities do you think children know?

Activity

Students should brainstorm a list of well-recognized and important people. It can be from government (like the president), sports, and entertainment, as well as a couple of noteworthy scientists or local heroes. Students should also include some famous historical figures (Abraham Lincoln, Martin Luther King) and some fictional characters elementary kids might know (Iron Man, Wonder Woman). Finally, include some marketing spokespeople, such as Ronald McDonald or Flo (the Progressive Insurance salesperson). Students should get the list down to about ten and then put together a compilation of pictures (without their names on the pics).

The students should now survey children under ten years old by showing each picture and seeing how many are identified successfully. Interviewers need to agree beforehand on a point system, such as two points for the name, one point for showing knowledge of who the person is but not knowing the name (saying Martin Luther King "is the 'I Have a Dream' man"), and zero for not knowing. The interviewers should give no hints or help.

Tally up the answers to see who is known best.

Follow-up Questions/Discussions

- Are the best-known people by children under ten generally celebrities, marketing spokespeople, or people who have done something for the community otherwise (like scientists)?
- Children are reflecting what society shows them. Are you happy with the order of how recognizable each kind of person or character is? If you consider that the ones children know are more likely to be role models, is this a good thing? What are the advantages and disadvantages of the people being best and least known by children?
- If scientists and others who do a lot for society, but don't really entertain us, are less well-known, what does this say about our values as a culture?
- Who do you think deserves more or less recognition and why?
- Look up popular heroes of the 1920s to see if they're similar to today's types of people.

Social Questions for Students

- Who are the most well-known people at your school? Is there a good balance between personalities and types, such as academic kids, athletes, and artists in terms of notoriety? If you could adjust who is recognized (such as in the school's newspaper, in announcements, or on its web page), how would you do it?

- Should everyone at your school be celebrated for something?

Lesson 6C—Drawing a Conclusion

Key Concepts
market penetration of children, cultural impression of children
Special Materials/Media
markers/crayons/colored pencils and paper
Intro Questions/Thoughts for Students

- What does it mean to "consume" something? What is a "consumer" in terms of shopping? Why do you think they are called "consumers"?
- How early do we become consumers? Can we be consumers, part of buying and selling, before we even realize it?
- Can you name brand names for things you don't consume yet but probably will in the future? Why or how do you know these brand names already?
- Can you "consume" information? How so?

Activity

This is a modified version of an actual study done by children's marketers to analyze **market penetration**. Students should ask a group of children (under ten years old) to close their eyes and imagine "shopping." Give the children a minute to sit in silence and picture whatever they see, and then have the students ask the children to draw what they pictured as best they can. Reassure the children it doesn't matter if the drawings are good or bad, as they will get a chance to explain their drawing. IMPORTANT: No clues or nudges should be given. If a child says, "Can I draw . . . ?" students should tell them to draw whatever they think of with "shopping," that there is no right or wrong.

As the children finish, they should be taken to another area and interviewed about what they drew. Students may point and ask, "What is this?" or "Why is that there?" but they should not suggest anything, such as asking, "Is that a Target logo?"

The researchers can then analyze the results with the follow-up questions as tabulating guides.

Follow-up Questions/Discussions

- When generally surveying children, researchers often prefer to have children draw and explain rather than just use words. Why do you think that is?

- What is the children's most common type of store (clothing, toys, food, online)?
- Are there any particular shopping centers, malls, or particular stores (by name) depicted? Even if the child is too young for the store or doesn't have money, why might this be good for the store? How do you think the child came to know that specific place or name?
- Any particular brands named? Why do you think that brand name became known?
- How often did the child portray themselves (or a child in general)? Is the child happy/sad about shopping? What do you think that reflects?
- How are adults, such as parents or store personnel, depicted?
- How often do the children show any awareness of money or cost, such as a sale price, a dollar sign, price tags, a cash register, or even the words "on sale"?
- Any trends in special fascinations for children, such as shopping carts, escalators, shopping bags, and so on? How much is online shopping portrayed?
- For all of the above, are there any general trend differences by gender? One such study found that boys saw shopping more as a utilitarian event (going to get what they want/need) while girls saw shopping as a pleasurable social experience unto itself. If you found that, why do you think there is that difference? Are boys and girls taught this difference?

Social Questions for Students

- For you, is shopping more just a method to get what you need/want, or it is a fun experience on its own, a social activity? Are there patterns among your peers as to who sees it one way or the other? Are those attitudes learned or taught?
- What do you take for granted about shopping or assume "everyone does" that someone your age from a different socioeconomic background might not?

Lesson 6D—Fun Me Downs

Key Concepts

belonging centric in children, indirect messaging from parents, cultural (tacit) pressure

Special Materials/Media

Access to Internet for research

Intro Questions/Thoughts for Students

- Were you given any toys or games, or introduced to them, by parents or older siblings who said, "I loved this as a kid!"?
- Did you ever feel pressure, even if it was not stated, to try or do something because it had been enjoyed by others before? Did you enjoy it?

Activity

Students think of toys or games that they had that have been around for a long time (if they cannot think of one, use Barbie dolls or construction sets). For whatever they pick, they should research the history of that toy: when it was invented, popularity, and how it looked and changed over the years. If it has been changed since they played with it, what are those changes? Students can then make a timeline of that toy, including placing their time playing with the toy on it. If their parents played with the toy or engaged in the activity, the student should place their parents in the timeline.

As a further challenge, students should imagine and design the "next generation" of that toy. What will it look like (or what extra features) do they imagine it will have in twenty years?

Follow-up Questions/Discussions

- If you enjoyed playing with that toy or activity, was part of the enjoyment knowing that you were doing something your parents (or older siblings) did?
- Were there any toys or activities handed down to you that you did not like? What happened? Did the older person try to talk you into liking it or "giving it another try"?
- Were you surprised by any of the changes of your toy over the years? Could you use the changes as part of a history report on how technology (such as the use of plastic) or society (Barbie as a housewife to astronaut) has changed over the years? For that matter, do you think toys reflect our society?
- As a follow-up activity, imagine five thousand years from now, archaeologists dig up the toys you have in your room. They don't know you, but what might they conclude about you, both rightly (from the game of Trouble, this kid liked to compete for fun) or wrongly (from Mouse Trap, this kid had a mouse problem in his bedroom or was training to be a professional mouse catcher)?
- As with hand-me-down toys, can ideas about things, like who/what is good, be passed down?

Social Questions for Students

- **Tacit pressure** is when you are not directly told to do something, but the circumstances try to nudge you to do it. If you walk into a library talking but then see people staring at you, you stop; this is tacit pressure, as no one directly told you to stop, but you got the message. Have you ever experienced tacit pressure to do or not do something? What about beliefs?

Lesson 6E—And We'll Have Fun, Fun, Fun till Daddy Takes the Toy-bird Away

Key Concepts
fun centric in children
Special Materials/Media
children to interview, access to Internet
Intro Questions/Thoughts for Students

- How do you define "fun"? Imagine a Martian coming to Earth and asking you to define this concept for her, not just with examples, but with a general definition that could cover all, but only, "fun" things.

Activity

The class should interview children (under ten) by asking what makes something "fun." Children can give an example, but follow up the example with "Why is that fun?"[6] Students then analyze the definitions or pictures gathered for trends, creating a checklist of things depicted or words used to indicate fun. Using the checklist items as parameters (factors that define a system, such as numbers or guidelines), students should then analyze activities or products advertised or promoted to children, such as day camps or toys. For each promotion, students should check off which parameters are met and how.

Follow-up Questions/Discussions

- Were there consistent adjectives or parameters for what is fun? From this, is there any way we can have a general, all-purpose definition of "fun"?
- Would children in other parts of the world (or across the country or city) agree with your interviewees' definition or examples of fun? Can you research toys from around the world and see if they meet the parameters you deduced for "fun"?

Social Questions for Students

- Has your definition of what makes something fun changed as you have gotten older? How so? Why do you think that has happened (or not)?
- Do you and your friends have similar or different definitions of fun? How so?

Lesson 6F—Older Younger

Key Concepts
aspirational thinking in children
Special Materials/Media
children to interview
Intro Questions/Thoughts for Students

- When you were under eight years old, what did you imagine you would be doing at this age now? How did you imagine school, sports, or activities? What is one thing you imagined and got right? What is one thing you imagined and were way off?
- Where do younger kids get their ideas of what being older is like?

Activity

Students should interview children under ten, asking them the open question of what they think life in middle school (or the interviewer's grade) will be like. If desired, this can be broken down into questions about school, sports, friends, and so on. The children should also be asked where they get their ideas of what middle school will be like. Finally, students should ask the children: if the child could own or do one thing that would make him or her "older" like a middle schooler, what would it be? Students should then tabulate and discuss results.

Follow-up Questions/Discussions

- As knowledgeable middle schoolers, were you surprised by the results of the children's depictions of middle school? What was accurate, and what was not? How does the accuracy of the current children's perception of middle school compare with what you had?
- How often did children mention the mundane, boring, or even bad parts of middle school, like homework, chores, or sitting on the bench?
- What about the one item? How many of you in your class have that item or agree that it would make middle school better?

- If children are perhaps getting an inaccurate or incomplete picture of life in middle school, do you think you are getting an incomplete idea of what high school or adulthood is like? How so?

Social Questions for Students

- Have you ever been caught in a situation you realized wasn't like you imagined it would be or weren't yet ready for?
- If you could give advice now to a child to help them have a better middle school experience, what would you say? Have you thought about what you can do now to make high school better for you?

Lesson 6G—From PG to G

Key Concepts
children's centrics
Special Materials/Media
None
Intro Questions/Thoughts for Students

- When you talk with someone, how do you adjust how you speak to them? What if it is an older or younger person, or someone who perhaps doesn't speak your language as well?
- Do you ever notice how adults and older people adjust the way they speak to you? Why do they do that?
- How do you adjust your body language and nonverbal communication in talking with others?

Activity

Students should think of things that are a part of middle-school life that aren't as common in elementary school. They can be fun (sports teams or dances), neutral (how to go through a cafeteria line or the school honor code), or some of the less fun aspects (homework).

Once the list is generated, students are divided into groups. They may pick something from the list or have one assigned. The group must then put together a thirty-second public service announcement (PSA) for children that informs them about that aspect of middle-school life. They can do it as a skit or as an ad, but they must intentionally incorporate all three of the children's centrics (belonging, fun, and aspiration) somewhere in the ad. The rest of the class should watch the performance and then try to guess where and how each centric was incorporated.

Follow-up Questions/Discussions

- When you acted out the centrics, did you intentionally make it obvious? On the one hand, children sometimes don't get a message unless you make it clear. On the other hand, have you ever rejected a message, even one you agreed with, because it was too "in your face"?
- If you addressed something that was bad, like tests or smelly locker rooms, was your message more "deal with it" or "make the best of it"? Why?
- See if your school will let you actually show the PSAs to the younger grades!

Social Questions for Students

- In the exercise, you adjusted your communication style for children. How do we adjust without being a "poser," condescending (speaking down to someone), or being something we are not? Why not one communication style for everyone?
- If you did a PSA about something unpleasant in middle school and conveyed the "make the best of it" approach, do you do this in real life? What is a bad situation you have that could benefit from a "make the best of it" approach by you?

Lesson 6H—Schooling You in Ads

Key Concepts
advertising penetration to children, establishing a brand as the **norm**
Special Materials/Media
trip to elementary school or division
Intro Questions/Thoughts for Students

- When given two different perspectives of a situation, one you've heard many times and one that is very different, do you treat them as having equal weight?
- How often are children exposed to ads? Are there any protected spaces from ads for children? Should there be?

Activity

Students should visit an elementary school or, if possible, shadow an elementary or kindergarten student at school. As the student does so, she should try to take note of all brands and logos that the child is exposed to. Differentiation should be in three types:

- brands and logos displayed by other children (such as on clothing or on their lunchboxes);
- brands and logos displayed directly by the company (billboard); and
- brands and logos that are displayed through the school (signs, scoreboards, lunchroom food, vending machines, lesson plans, busses, etc.).

Follow-up Questions/Discussions

- What was the most common source for the ads: the companies, peers, or the school?
- If children don't have a lot of money, why is it worth it for companies to advertise to them?
- If one sees one brand associated with one kind of a product, it becomes the **norm** for that product, which gives it an advantage (shoppers might think other brands are "off," "inferior," or "weird"). Do displays early in childhood help make some brands norms?
- Should schools be allowed to advertise? On the one hand, schools need money; on the other hand, the children are a "captured audience" who have no choice. Have a class debate on the topic.
- You did this experiment looking at a school or space other than your own. Repeat the exercise now with your own education space. Do you see ads and other things you didn't notice before?

Social Questions for Students

- Does norming or normalizing a brand work for ideas, too? If a child hears one point of view all the time, does that become the normal point of view and have greater weight than an opposing view? What ideas were made norms for you? What continues to be messaged to you?
- What social norms ("that's the way it is") do you not like? How could you "counter-norm" them? How could you send messages to convey another point of view?
- Have you ever said something to another person, presuming her life was the same as yours, only to find out she had a different experience? What social norms were you exposed to as children that may not be true in other places or not be true any longer?
- Find someone in the class who has a different point of view as you do on a topic. Each of you should take up to two minutes to express your opinion, and then each should get two additional minutes to say what you have in common or like about the other person's position. (You don't have to leave agreeing, but saying, "I think we are both passionate and care about it," is a start.)

NOTES

1. The first people to coin the term "centrics" in terms of marketing motivators may have been David Siegel, Timothy Coffey, and Gregory Livingston in their book *The Great Tween Buying Machine: Marketing to Today's Tweens* (Ithaca, NY: Paramount Market Publishing, 2001). They defined centrics, at least regarding tweens, as the "core drivers that motivate . . . behavior" (50). We use it here similarly, except with more focus on such "drivers" then becoming vulnerabilities by which media and messaging might resonate, persuade, and perhaps even manipulate us, for good or for bad. Alternatively, we define "drivers" as the deeper, subconscious psychological needs that coalesce into centrics. See chapter 7, lesson 7B.

2. Other than that it's a requirement of Texas citizenship to work it into all conversations with non-Texans.

3. James U. McNeal, *Kids as Customers: A Handbook of Marketing to Children* (New York: Lexington Books, 1992), 14–17.

4. Gary Ruskin, "Why They Whine: How Corporations Prey on Our Children," *Mothering Magazine*, July 1, 2003, http://www.mothering.com/10-0-0/html/10-3-0/10-3-whine97.shtml.

5. An interesting contrast is that, whereas tweens respond to pitches because they want to be part of this amorphous thing called "coolness" (whether or not they personally like it), children want cool only if it is fun to be so, which in essence means children are savvier consumers than tweens, as they are looking at coolness for its personal **utility** rather than its **panache**. See chapter 2 on **utility** and 4 on coolness and **panache**.

6. Alternatively, students can repeat the procedure in lesson 6C by asking children to draw what is "fun."

Chapter Seven

Tween Centrics

There are plenty of movies that tap into adult nostalgia for their free-wheeling college days and even a good many movies about reliving the good and bad of high school. There is virtually no market for movies, however, about going back to middle school/junior high. When that age is treated, it's either looking at the pain, struggle, and confusion of those years or about the joy of escaping from the daily struggles at that age.

The pre- and newly adolescent years—roughly about nine to twelve or thirteen years old—are collectively called the tween years because most kids feel awkwardly in between two states of being. While children, they operated in a world largely (and blissfully) separated from reality: everyone's a winner and a friend (except the bad guy that's always bested), the pie is always big enough if we just figure out how to share it, and success is our destiny. Then we hit the middle-school years, and the bubbles burst one by one: not everyone wins (some are just bad at things and no montage of practicing over and over again, like in a movie, can make them that much better). School is suddenly harder, the homework more challenging, and not everyone receives good grades. Worst of all, the tween's place in the world is starting to come into view, as the tween realizes he or she is near the bottom of the power pyramid.

Still, the tween years are also exciting, as young people discover they have new powers, and the greater freedom and messiness of reality can be exhilarating. If childhood is a fantasy world, tween years are augmented reality;[1] if childhood is a game that requires strictly sticking to a board game path and seeing who is first to go around to the finish, the tween years are an open-world video game where the side tasks and main quest unfold slowly and don't necessarily have a precise order.

See Lesson 7A—Game On!

A good media distinction between childhood and tween years is *Scooby Doo* versus *Harry Potter*. The *Scooby Doo* gang of teens, along with Scooby the dog, has been solving mysteries since 1969, almost fifty years (or almost 350 Scooby years). Most younger children identify with Shaggy, the goofy member who only really connects with his best friend, Scooby Doo the dog. Shaggy is the least powerful of the humans, seemingly discounted by the rest, as he and Scooby are usually sent off by themselves. They are the most afraid of whatever mystery is afoot, and they often mess up the trap. Yet, they are the ones, even accidentally, who lead the "monster" to being caught, at which time it is revealed, reassuringly, that there are no real monsters, just bad people, who always see justice delivered . . . a fairy tale with a happy ending.

In contrast, *Harry Potter* is, even in fantasy form, the epitome of tween life. There, young people discover at around age eleven that they are not what they thought (at least in Harry's case), that they have new, incredible powers and must learn how to use them. Their new environment (Hogwarts) is strange and full of mysteries, as are their classmates. Not all children are the same or friends, and some are even bad (and not the kind of bad that, if we just get to know each other, we'll realize we're really all the same).

There are romances and the confusion of figuring out where one fits in. There is the potential for doing cool things one could never do before, but there is also very real, and very adult, danger that must be confronted and dealt with, and not with a completely happy ending, even if they do prevail. The world of *Harry Potter* is big, messy, dangerous, empowering, and exciting, but new entrants must learn fast or face failure. Welcome to the tween years!

As with children's marketing and messaging, it's helpful to see what those who want to influence tweens say are the resonating appeals, or, again, centrics, so that tweens can be better prepared to understand why they respond to messaging as they do (even without consciously knowing). It's hard to find marketing venturers willing to explore a tween's mind, filled with a maze of twisty little passages, all different,[2] but one such group of intrepid explorers was David Siegel, Timothy Coffey, and Gregory Livingston, who wrote *The Great Tween Buying Machine*,[3] a marketing guide for similarly bent folks. As McNeal did for children, Siegel et al. did for the middle phase of childhood, and so many media lit lessons are made with their research and revelations in mind.

Drawing on the pioneer work of Swiss psychologist and child development expert Jean Piaget (who, if he were alive today, would no doubt be not too pleased that his studies are used to sell children yogurt-in-a-tube), Siegel and crew divide the tween years into two phases, that of being an *emerging tween* (roughly from ages nine to ten) and that of being a *transitioning tween* (eleven to twelve).[4] In both phases, the tween stands astride two tectonic plates, like California, trying to keep one's footing even as the ground shifts in two directions. For the emerging tween, she is standing in both the concreteness of childhood and the abstract ambiguity of adolescence; for the transitioning tween, he is standing astride the ambiguity of adolescence and the slightly more fixed, but not yet adult, world of teenage-dom.

As emerging tweens, young people are starting to realize that the world is not merely a wonderland of causal connection but has an order, albeit a rough one, and that things within the world have different valuations. Tweens this age are still largely concrete thinkers, but they are beginning to see patterns in the ranking and valuation of things. Siegel[5] calls these searches for logical placement **seriation** (putting things in order) and **classification** (assigning relative value).[6] It is one of the first ways young people begin to try to understand messaging on their own (as opposed to either taking it as all true or accepting a parent's, teacher's, or other authority figure's valuation of the message).

Tweens yearn for such systems to superimpose artificial order on the chaotic inundation of information, reducing life to manageable boxes. This, perhaps, explains why cliques become important in middle school for many students. Faced with the new information that some students prefer or are good at some things while others are not, tweens look to assemble and categorize people by a single characteristic: the jocks, the social kids, the computer geeks, and so on. Of course, while this kind of information processing helps tweens to digest complex reality initially, if it becomes a non-evolving fixed perspective, it can become detrimental to understanding overlap and nuance later in life.

The tendency for seriation and classification is also evident in younger tweens' desires for collecting things, from tangible trading cards to pixelated achievement trophies in video games. In whatever activity they like, tweens feel like they've "gotta catch 'em all" (a brilliant phrase that both summed up the Pokémon experience and acted as a marketing nudge for children and tweens to keep buying more!).

And then it hits. If you are a sixth- or seventh-grade teacher, you know what "it" is. Neither Bruce Banner being bombarded with gamma rays into the Hulk, nor an atomic spider bite transforming Peter Parker into Spider-Man, compares with the transformation caused by the hormonal rush we reduce to a single word: *puberty*.[7] One day Johnny is an angel who helps pass out papers; next week he's pulling up the carpet because he's bored or teasing Nadia because he wants her attention. The truest answer any kid this age gives in response to "Why did you do that?" is "I dunno."

For tweens at this tumultuous time, their heretofore primary sources for information, truth, and moral guidance—aka Mom, Dad, and teachers—become less relied upon. Pubescent tweens are likely to withhold information from parents, not so much out of loss of faith in parental knowledge, but as a transition into their own self-exploration for an independent identity.

As the tweens are letting go of allowing Mom and/or Dad to be at the helm, they are becoming self-propelling (or at least now allowing internal forces in their brain and body to guide the ship). Siegel refers to four **drivers** that subconsciously propel newly pubescent tweens in their information processing and valuation of the world.[8] They also might be called "proto-centrics," as they are the deeper, subconscious psychological impulses that coalesce into more complicated centrics:

1. fun
2. power
3. freedom
4. belonging

Fun is placed first because this represents a holdover from childhood. It's also the least "social," as fun is often self-determined. As the tween courses through her pubescent transition, however, she starts to reflect and measure herself more in relation to others. Thus, if one wants to reach a tween with a message, the younger, still emerging tween will respond to a "this is fun" nudge while the older, transitioning tween will respond more to an "everyone is doing it" nudge.

These drivers, or proto-centrics, remain somewhat ambiguous, subject to many interpretations (freedom from what? parents? rules? baths?), and whether an image represents one driver or another is often a subjective call (Is a picture of a group of tweens shopping together "freedom" to choose what they want or "belonging" in a group activity?). Still, media lit is more focused on awakening young people to these potential internal drivers than precisely defining driver boundaries.

See Lesson 7B—Who's in the Driver's Seat?

See Lesson 7C—Driving Home the Point

For the transitioning, older tweens, their worst fear is to be regarded as, or grouped with, emerging tweens. They would much rather be at the bottom of the teen/future adult hierarchy than at the top of the child/young tween one. Many K–12 schools have begun programming in the past decade to bring students from the entire school together (rather than have three divisions of elementary, middle, and upper schools). Often students are grouped in "families," "cohorts," or "legacy groups" with each group having two to three members from each grade who do an activity together, usually one more geared toward the younger kids for their sake.

Invariably, older students will play with the little kids (once the high schoolers put away their AP books), the little kids will look in awe at the older ones, but what of the sixth, seventh, and eighth graders? They will stay on the sidelines, sitting and watching or, perhaps, trying to do their own thing among themselves. They almost never want to do (let alone enjoy) what they see as a little kid activity, even if their high school role models are doing it. Puberty is like Caesar's Rubicon river: once crossed, there is no going back, at least until one is comfortable enough with oneself to dance like an uninhibited child (usually around the time one acquires grandchildren).

See Lesson 7D—Judging a Book by Its Cover

In a world they now see as composed of many types of people with many different roles, the transitioning tween is compelled to wonder what their role will be. To know that, however, they have to figure out who they are. This drives tweens into an egoism, not one of vanity, but of unsure self-discovery.

As part of a diversity self-assessment at our school, middle-school students were asked to describe where they saw themselves fitting in and how confident they felt about their role. Unsurprisingly, most fourth and even fifth graders felt pretty good about themselves and where they fit in. Sixth and seventh graders, however, saw a precipitous drop in self-assuredness, either in defining one's self or in how confident they felt about themselves fitting into school culture. By eighth grade, however, there was a distinct trend back up, especially in self-confidence as to having (or not) a definitive role in school, a sort of "I'm still not sure who I am, but I'm OK with it" mindset.

In addressing media lit issues with students in the face of such tween egoism, the teacher is challenged in several ways. First, students may be uncomfortable analyzing data, as the explorations are touching upon these new, sensitive areas ("Stop talking to me about me! I'm too busy trying to figure me out, so I just want to focus on me . . . alone!").

Second, as we will see, tweens have a lot of contrasting centrics all fighting to be the dominant motivator. A tween may want to give the right answer to show mastery, but they also want to be independent and not just someone who does what the teacher says (and who gets admired for that?), but then again, they don't want to be *too* noticed and sticking out because that won't be accepted by the group. Like we said, few people fondly reminisce about navigating the level 6 rapids of sixth grade. It's important, then, for the teacher to make sure to reinforce some ground rules to reassure students:

- The lessons are not talking about any individual student. Like all behavioral economics, a single case is rarely worth anything (called the fallacy of **anecdotal evidence**). Even if we ask a student for her opinion or how he feels, it is only to add it into the greater mix and see what the data shows about the greater trend.
- No one is to be made fun of because of what he says, nor should anyone have to respond or reveal something she does not wish to reveal.
- When doing any kind of psychological or sociological study of one's own group, it is very common to have an "Oh my gosh—that's me!" reaction (first-year psychology majors are notorious for self-diagnosing themselves as having every disorder they study). Everyone will probably relate at least a little bit to the ideas and feelings being investigated.
- These lessons and exercises are not to say, "Don't do it," or that advertisers or messengers who use these techniques are bad or wrong. They are merely so that the students can be aware of what is being used to persuade them. It's OK to want to do something in part to be popular or for any other centric; just maybe don't overdo it!
- Have fun with it. It's serious stuff, as businesses spend billions of dollars to do all this, but that doesn't mean we can't have fun figuring it out like detectives.

The centrics here were born of ad men trying to sell products to kids, but they are also the vehicles by which ideas, points of view, and world outlooks are delivered as well. We follow up all of the exercises involving marketing with questions to get the kids to think of how their opinions and perspectives are similarly affected, and in many ways that follow-up is more important, for while tweens know they are buying products, like clothes, which they will probably discard once they grow out of them, they are not aware that they are also picking up points of view that they may carry with them the rest of their lives.

As another methodological tip to teachers, a great way to get this age interested is to tap into the centrics themselves for your own use, such as *mastery*. As you'll see below, kids love being able to see what adults (like marketers) are trying to do and saying, "Hah, I see what you are doing!" Shhh, we won't tell the kids you're using the techniques to teach the techniques.[9]

Turning back to our trusted guide, Siegel, he and his fellow marketers have broken down the tween full-blown centrics, which we feel are more apt for the transitioning tween, into seven touchpoints:[10]

1. worth
2. mastery
3. individuality

4. imagination
5. popularity
6. friendship
7. superiority

All of these are generally positive attributes and desires we would want to encourage tweens to develop, but like a pinch of salt in a recipe, we have to be careful not to add too much, and we should look for how much is also hidden in so many other things that can accumulate to cause high blood pressure. So yeah, this is where we have to be the "negative Neds" who say, "Yes, it's great, but . . . "

WORTH

Every child should feel special and valued; then again, many a coach will tell you the downfall of a team begins when their star player comes to embrace their specialness too much. It's a fine line for a parent between building up their child's self-esteem and overinflating his ego. It's less of a problem for marketers, who don't have to live with the results.

While counterintuitive to think someone would believe a message from someone they've never met, broadcast to millions of people, affirming that she is "special," kids buy into such messages every day and buy the product (or message) that seems to be just for someone of their specialness. Many products include flattering, ego-inflating statements such as "because you're worth it," and many arguments have an undertone of "You're one of the smart ones, so you know I'm right!"

For tweens, who are in a new, unsure place in their lives as they wrestle with their new powers and problems, a flattering message draws them in, like a reassuring safe port in a storm. Unfortunately, the safety may only be illusory in that an appeal to a tween's worth can set up unrealistic expectations. If every tween assumes they are Roald Dahl's "Charlie" and it's their destiny to find the golden ticket and end up owning the chocolate factory, are they prepared for the occasions when they are not so special and don't win?

Tweens can also fall prey to contests and games where, despite the odds, they just "know" they will win. Even more, the worth hook is one that's hard to remove. The consumption of the product, or the agreeing with the particular point of view, is the confirmation of worth, and so to reject that product or idea is tantamount to saying, "I'm not worthy." The tween's worth is then deeply tied to what product he possesses or point of view she espouses, not who he or she is.

See **Lesson 7E—You're Special . . . Every Single One of You**

MASTERY

Accomplishment is the key to true self-esteem, so how can an emphasis on accomplishing things, or encouraging tweens to do so, be potentially bad for them? Like anything else, it's a matter of balance. If winning is the goal, we sometimes lose sight of what it may cost to get there, and tweens can be pretty focused on proving they can do it no matter the cost.

Down here in Texas, the world stops for a couple of weeks in October for the State Fair in Dallas. The Midway, with all its carny games, becomes overrun with tweens, who will spend fifty dollars to win a fifty-cent stuffed animal. There's also the issue of process versus result. For many ads and entertainment shows, the process of self-improvement has a definite end goal (whatever the contest being prepped for), and the process is worth little if they do not win.

See **Lesson 7F—"A Work in Process"**

INDIVIDUALITY

Raise your hand if you are an individual who doesn't follow what other people say for you to do! Gotcha!

Everyone is unique and adds something to the mix. At the beginning of last chapter, we mentioned the Greek philosopher Heraclitus, who said we never step in the same river twice, as the river always changes. What we forget is that the river is not the same, in part, because we stepped in it. In the legal world, any time a partner is added to or taken away from a firm, it is as if the old partnership dies and a new one is instantly born of the new members. We are impactful, and that's good for tweens to hear.[11]

At the same time, it's getting harder and harder to stand out. In many ways this is good. When one considers how, fifty years ago, the boy who dared to have his hair touch the back of his collar was considered an upstart rebel who would bring down the entire educational system.

Today, we're more relaxed and waste less of our time on such existential threats to Western civilization. But for the kids who desperately want to stand out, where do they go? What extremes (and potential dangers) do they have to go to that are not only true individuality but a type where other kids won't say, "I already saw that in a movie"? How much money must a young person spend, or what acts must be done or outlandish ideas proclaimed, for them to get a "that's different" affirmation?

We in American culture love the rebel, the cowboy who weighs matters by his or her own personal scales of justice, tossing away societal convention with "Sometimes, ya gotta break the rules." Marketers tap into this rebellion by telling potential consumers that their products or ideas are great simply because they disrupt the system (and what tween doesn't want to do a little disruption?), but we also like a whole bunch of rules and norms we take for granted.

No one would be OK with a driver cruising down the wrong side of the street yelling, "Ya gotta break the rules," and if we all break the rules, who is left? Would we be OK if all the lunchroom staff took the day off without telling anyone or with the folks who supply electricity deciding to not bother? That's a question that is beyond the scope of most ads and many programs: when is thoughtful bending or breaking the rules warranted and admirable, and when is it, well, just dumb?

***See* Lesson 7G—Breaking the Rule Breakers**

IMAGINATION

"What if . . . ?" may be one of the best, most fun questions we get to ask at any age, let alone by tweens who are seeing the world with fresh eyes. They are unburdened by layers of presumption or memories of trying an approach that didn't work before. It's hard for marketers and messengers to mess up this one, but they can.

Imagining new things is hard to do,[12] and for a tween who doesn't yet have the confidence to promote something truly new, it is sometimes safer to stick with what's been done. This can lead to "pre-packaged" imagination that, while a good start, should not be the end point.[13] On the other hand, imagination is great, but is it enough to get the full picture? Marketers glamorize certain professions (rock stars) and ignore others (researcher), and this can have an effect on kids' aspirations, not to mention their valuation of peers and their varied talents.

***See* Lesson 7H—Change the Story**

POPULARITY

Everyone wants to be liked, if not by everyone, then by people we are close to or respect, famously captured with Sally Field's "You like me!" 1985 Oscar awards speech.[14] In tween terms, popularity is like the culmination of worth and mastery; it's the affirmation that, even if a tween's ego is built upon an unsure foundation about herself, popularity is the flying buttress that keeps her ego edifice propped up. Marketers know this is an exceptional centric that kids will embrace, along with the products that purport to bring them popularity. All the while, teachers know this can be one of the biggest problem-causers in school.

What will a tween do for the ephemeral moment of all eyes on them? What are the kids (and sometimes their parents) willing to spend to buy admiration; what is a class clown willing to do to be thought funny; and above all, how do the kids learn the difference between being temporarily liked for what someone possesses or says or does versus being authentically and lastingly appreciated for who they are?

However difficult this challenge is for tangible goods, it can be worse when dealing with intangible, but popular, ideas. If a certain skill is popular (such as sports or gaming), how do we feel about those who don't do it? If most everyone feels a certain way about an issue, how does the person who has a different view feel about expressing a differing opinion?

***See* Lesson 7I—Cool Pops**

FRIENDSHIP

Humans are social animals, and friends are our comforting pack. We get reinforced we're OK by our friends' similar lives, and if people think the same way, it's OK for us to do so. So how can a marketer or messenger exploit this? Consider the message to a group of tweens, "If you were all friends, you would . . . " This could be good (" . . . look out for each other," or " . . . care about each other."), but if it was followed by " . . . wear the same clothes as sold by . . . " it no longer appears to be addressing positive values so much as positive sales.

This can also apply to ideas or attitudes ("If you were my friend, you would not be friends with him"). Now we're getting into the power/manipulation side that constitutes emotional blackmail. The other aspect of this is that the friendship tug is like gravity. Jupiter is a lot bigger than the person next to you, but that person's proximity makes their gravitational pull stronger on you. A tween can get a lot of messages to choose one path ("Don't smoke"), but a single friend with another message ("Try it once; what can it hurt?") can make them go the other way.

See Lesson 7J—Against the Grain

SUPERIORITY

Back in 1993, when the World Wide Web was first opening up, *The New Yorker* magazine published a presentient cartoon of two dogs sitting in front of a desktop computer, with one saying, "On the Internet, nobody knows you're a dog." True then; truer now.

Today, tweens are starting to play in the adult world, and vice versa. No one knows if you are a tween playing online poker for money or a thirty-year-old playing an MMORPG[15] against kids (or a media lit textbook writer taking a quick break). Tweens are competing and they want to win, but do they have the maturity to know how to deal with winning, especially in an adult-infused world?

This centric is similar to mastery, but whereas mastery's challenge is about dealing with what to do when one doesn't win, superiority is more about appreciating and maintaining civility when one is one step higher than others on the podium. Tweens are notoriously short-term consequence thinkers, so overenjoying the moment of victory, especially by belittling the competition, may have "what goes around, comes around" escalating consequences. What happens when today's winner loses? How will they be treated? What happens if the person you belittle today is on your team tomorrow?

See Lesson 7K—Sore Winner

There are more centrics revolving around the tween years because there is so much transition going on in such a short time. It's no wonder that, in the teaching world, if a teacher says they teach elementary school, they get a smile; if they say they teach high school, they get an amused head shake; but if they say they teach middle school, they get a hug and a "God bless you!"

See Lesson 7L—Cen-tricks of the Trade

One last facet regarding the desires of transitioning tweens and their focus bears investigation, especially for teachers of seventh and eighth graders. At some point, tweens are done with the transitioning process and are ready and eager to get on to the next stage of life, that of being a teenager. Because of this, they engage, as children do, in **aspirational thinking** and desires, or in plainer language, wanting to be more grown up.

Specifically, tweens start to adjust their world view relative to two distinct groups "above" them. First, tweens become fascinated with and desirous of teen culture. They love TV shows about high school life, often seeing them as prep manuals for future fun. Not content to just watch from afar, transitioning tweens then try to imitate teen life, whether the fashion, the attitude, or the lifestyle they think of as "cool teen." Unfortunately, this can lead to tweens embracing aspects of life they are not ready for, or in media lit terms, **KGOY**, Kids Getting Older Younger.

See **Lesson 7M—Teen Romance**

The other group tweens compare themselves with is the adults, more particularly parents, teachers, and other people in seeming authority. The key word for a tween is "seeming," as tweens want to show these adults that they can hold their own in an adult world. This is why we often see adults in tween-oriented shows as goofy, somewhat clueless, and fooled by tweens (this is as opposed to teen shows, where adults are generally not present or minimally present). Tweens love the power in reversing the roles by them teaching adults, or at least influencing adults' lives. In terms of consumerism, marketers directly play to this, even dubbing this kind of nudge on parental decisions the "nag factor."[16]

See **Lesson 7N—Adult or a Dolt?**

TEEN CENTRICS

> When I was a boy of fourteen, my father was so ignorant I could hardly stand to have the old man around. But when I got to be twenty-one, I was astonished at how much the old man had learned in seven years.—Mark Twain

Mark Twain captured the essence of both being a young teen and how insufferable they can be to adults, seemingly approaching simple situations with a combination of arrogance and ignorance, with often just a soupcon of hyper-emotion. There is no eighth-grade teacher who hasn't thought at some point, "This part of the lesson was only supposed to take five minutes; why are we doing it the hard way?!"

Still, if Twain's teen self were to reflect on middle-school years, he might have said, "When I was a boy of ten, my middle-school teachers were so elementary that I could hardly stand how simplistic and black-and-white they portrayed the world. But when I got to be thirteen, I was astonished at how they had learned to consider interesting abstract ideas about the world beyond our bubble."

In the context of how to teach students this age, and especially as regards processing the messages of the newly entered world of young adulthood, they are doing the best they can with brains that aren't developing evenly all at once, like if their forearms grew first and then the upper arms caught up.

So, let's start with the frightening, but necessary, trip into a young teen's brain.

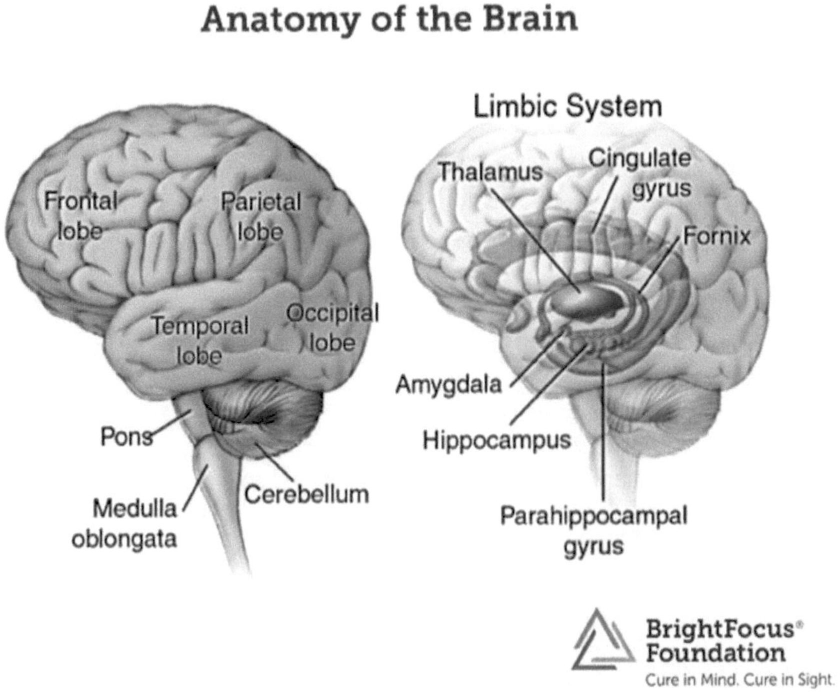

Anatomy of the brain. BrightFocus Foundation, Anatomy of the Brain, 2000, https://www.brightfocus.org/alzheimers/infographic/brain-anatomy-and-limbic-system.

With the onset of puberty, the brain starts to be driven by the limbic system and its hormonal bath of emotions. In this drive, there is clearly a lead chauffeur, a tiny, almond-shaped sliver of the brain called the *amygdala*. It is the hormonal screamer in the otherwise quiet restaurant of the mind. It's the one that hears the teacher say, "You didn't quite get that correct," and screams back, "You hate me!" or who replies to a parent saying the family is having dinner together with "You're ruining my life!"

In adults, the counterbalance to the emotional overreaction is provided by the prefrontal cortex. Unfortunately, neuroscience suggests that this part of the brain does not fully develop until about age twenty-five, meaning that for at least ten years, a young adult's brain is being driven by a mad, crazed, impulsive amygdala with the prefrontal cortex in the passenger seat whispering, "Please stop, that's not a good idea."

This is the playing field not only for young teen education, but for them to receive and process the messages they are being exposed to by society. They know they are in a different place than where they were a year or two ago, and they know they are a different person in many ways trying to process the change, a walking experiment with multiple independent variables. In a sense, it's also not unlike when an adult visits a country or culture very different from their own; one becomes overly sensitive with reading cues and not violating norms and believes everyone is looking at them and judging them negatively![17]

***See* Lesson 7O—Gnothi Seauton**

CHAPTER 7 ACCOMPANYING LESSONS

Lesson 7A—Game On!

Key Concepts

complexity of life as a tween, abstractly rendered

Special Materials/Media

poster board, markers, random materials that can be used with board games (dice, moving pieces), ability to print pictures to attach to board game

Intro Questions/Thoughts for Students

- Do you feel your life is more complicated as a tween than when you were in elementary school? How so?
- Do you have to make more daily decisions that change your day now than you did as a child? How so? Do you like making more decisions?

Activity

In groups, students plot out a "typical day" of being a tween. It can be a school day or a weekend, but students should discuss and plan out a day (or week if they want a longer period with more material) of the traps and boons that are typical and come along fairly regularly. Using this information, each group should then create a board game that is a "path game" (like Candyland) but based on the hazards and helps of tween life. They should decorate the board to suit, printing off pictures that reflect the hazards and helps of the game.

In conjunction with a writing assignment, the group must write out the rules so clearly that people could play the game without assistance from the game makers. Students then play each other's games and discuss what each put in or left out.

Follow-up Questions/Discussions

- In what way were the games accurate of tween life and not?

- If elementary children were to play your game, what parts would they be already familiar with, what parts might they have heard about, and what parts would be new?
- Was there anything you thought of but intentionally left off? Why?
- Do you think it would help rising tweens to play your game ahead of time?

Social Questions for Students

- Was it fun to discuss the common problems and potential hazards of tween life? Why was that? Do you think it would be helpful to regularly talk about challenges of tween life with each other?
- If you could give one bit of advice to next year's student in your current grade, what would you say? What is the biggest hazard? The best benefit?
- If your parents saw the game (or the decorations), what parts would surprise them? Why do you think they don't know? Should they know?
- Was there anything that is a big part of tween life but you couldn't express it?

Lesson 7B—Who's in the Driver's Seat?

Key Concepts

four "drivers" (individuality, fun, belonging, and empowerment) of tween information processing and valuation

Special Materials/Media

posters, magazines (to make collages)

Intro Questions/Thoughts for Students

- What are the biggest motivators in your life? Success? Fun? Approval?
- Fill in the blanks: Most of all, I want to be ________________ in life! I would like others to feel ____________ toward me.

Activity

This is a modified version of a study done by actual tween marketers.[18] The class makes four collages of pictures from magazines they feel represent one of the following four words: individuality, fun, belonging, and empowerment (these words are not on the posters).

The posters are shown to tweens who answer the following questions:

- Which poster (marked A, B, C, and D) best reflects how you see yourself?
- Which poster best depicts "success"?

The tween-respondents should then be asked, separately from the posters, about the words themselves (on a second sheet of paper so tweens can't see the words before they complete task 1), asking them to rank the four words as to how much they accurately describe themselves and successful people. Surveyors should be sure to note the age (and if desired, gender) of the respondents on the surveys.

Fun

Freedom/Individuality

Power

Belonging

Follow-up Questions/Discussions

- Did the valuation of the posters generally agree with the valuation of the words themselves? If they did not, what might that tell you about the posters as reflecting the values?
- If you divided the responses into two groups, ages 9–10 and 11–13, do you find a big difference in the valuation?
- From an experiment point of view, why was it important to not show respondents the words themselves before they had completed the poster part of the experiment?
- Also, from an experiment point of view, does it matter whether you were interviewing someone you knew or did not know? Might some responses be given to "look good" (**posing**) rather than because that is what the respondent honestly felt?
- How many respondents see themselves as aligning with "success"? What can you interpret from the results? Do most tweens think they are currently valuing what leads to success? Is this important?

Social Questions for Students

- Do you think you are on a path to success? How do you define "success"? Do you think that definition changes over time? How much of your definition of "success" is yours versus your parents', the school's, or somebody else's? How much should you consider someone else's definition of success?
- Is it OK to just want one of these values, such as friendship, and not care about the others? Is it OK to not care about *any* of these values? Is it OK to have *no* particular goal at all (to just want "to be")?

Lesson 7C—Driving Home the Point

Key Concepts

use of the four "drivers" (individuality, fun, belonging, and empowerment) of tween information processing and valuation in persuasive messaging to tweens

Special Materials/Media

Access to Internet for research, copying pictures, and creating ads

Intro Questions/Thoughts for Students

- How do marketers and other messengers to tweens appeal to your feelings in order to persuade you? How can they do it through imagery?

Activity

For the four drivers—individuality, fun, belonging, and empowerment—the class should collectively brainstorm brands or products that they most associate with each. Once a list is generated, the class is divided into four groups, with each group assigned one of the drivers. They are to research ads for the brands and products just listed for how their driver is invoked or represented (or see if another driver seemingly is). They should copy and paste the pictures they find (or capture from TV ads) to show how the driver is depicted.

As added fun, the teacher should pick out an ordinary product (such as a toothbrush, duct tape, or healthy snack). Each group must either design a poster ad or act out a thirty-second commercial that uses their driver to sell the product to tweens.

Follow-up Questions/Discussions

- What do you think of the brands associated with a particular value? Do you agree? Do you see any brands double listed?
- Do you think the brand makers like being thought of with that driver? Do you think the brands intentionally try to be seen that way? Why?

Social Questions for Students

- How much do you think you are affected by surrounding images as you judge something's worth? If you see someone surrounded by admiring people, would you think of them the same way compared to them dressed and acting the exact same way but standing alone?
- Is it OK to like people simply because they admire you?

Lesson 7D—Judging a Book by Its Cover

Key Concepts

packaging as messaging for tweens

Special Materials/Media

Access to Internet, materials to make and decorate packaging

Intro Questions/Thoughts for Students

- Have you ever stopped and looked at a product on sale because the packaging caught your eye (it had **eye appeal**)?
- How much does a product's packaging affect your decision to buy it? If you are not sure about buying a product, can packaging be a tipping point/deciding factor? What about between two brands for the same product?

- Do you think that marketers change the packaging for different groups? How so?

Activity

Students should think of products that are either used by kids of all ages (like shampoo) or are used much more by one age group than another (bubble gum or games versus make-up). If possible, try to separate products predominantly sold to those ten and younger and those sold to kids eleven and older. Students should look at the packaging for those products (not the separate ads or the product itself), comparing the packaging for:

- use of color, both as background and in lettering;
- simplicity versus complexity (including words);
- playfulness (does the package look like an animal or more grown up?); and
- people on the package (and their expressions).

Students should then create a comparison list of "rules of packaging" for the two groups as a chart:

	Rule for ten and under packaging	Rule for eleven and older packaging
colors		
words		
playfulness		
people		

Given these rules, the students are put into two teams, one for each age group, and assigned an everyday product (such as a stapler or backpack). Using a cardboard box (it doesn't matter if it is too small to actually hold the product, as it is a model), the teams must design the packaging for that product.

Follow-up Questions/Discussions

- What kind of messages did you see implied in the packaging? Do you see the four drivers discussed previously in the packaging (such as people having fun together to imply friendship or belonging)?
- If marketers change the packaging of physical products, do people also change the "packaging" of messages for the different age groups? For a

message of "Don't do drugs" or "Be friends; don't exclude," how might the "packaging" (how the message is conveyed) differ?

Social Questions for Students

- Do you ever "package" yourself? You are the same person, but how do you change the outside or your look to fit different occasions?
- What do you think of the phrase "A new look leads to a new *you*"?
- There is "deceptive advertising" in product packaging; can there be the same idea in how humans "package" themselves?

Lesson 7E—You're Special . . . Every Single One of You

Key Concepts

tween centric of worth, persuasion through **flattery**

Special Materials/Media

Access to Internet

Intro Questions/Thoughts for Students

- How many stories can you think of in which a young person discovers he or she is not ordinary but is "special" in terms of powers?
- If someone said you were "special," what does that mean to you? Do you like being told you are special? Is there ever a time you don't like it? Besides compliments, what are ways other people compliment you or make you feel special (such as likes on social media)?
- If someone compliments you, do you think that affects the way you then feel about them? Does it matter if the compliment is just to you or is said to a lot of people?

Activity

Students should first discuss ways people show they think another person has worth, from word compliments ("you're awesome"), to actions (helping someone), to gestures (nodding or thumbs up), to special symbols ("likes," emojis). Once a list is compiled, students should look for ads that show these four kinds of *affirmations* (emotional support or encouragement). The target of the affirmation can also be divided into three groups:

- the ad viewer ("Because you're worth it . . . ");
- a **viewer substitute** (a person in the ad who is like the probable viewer, like a tween, so that the viewer can put themselves in their place, such as saying, "For active, fun people" while showing such); and
- another kind of person.

Follow-up Questions/Discussions

- Why do ads try to compliment and build up the viewer's ego?
- Which of the four kinds of affirmations did you see most in ads? Why do you think that is? Does that reflect what you experience in real life?
- Of the three types of people, who was the most common object of the affirmations? Why do you think that was?
- If a seller is telling you that you should use their product because you are a leader, because you're athletic, or "because you're worth it," is there an implication that to not use their product is to say you are not that way?
- It is easier to see marketers using **flattery** (excessive and insincere praise) in ads, but do other messengers use it too ("You're smart; you must see I'm right!")?

Social Questions for Students

- Is there potential long-term harm of building up a person's ego by telling her she is "special"? What is the balance between building self-esteem and realistic expectations?
- We should listen to others as they can give feedback as part of a community, but how much should one's self-worth be determined by others' approval?
- Of the four kinds of affirmations above, which are the hardest to do? Is it easier to click like or to help someone out? Which is the most meaningful way for you to be affirmed?
- Is it OK to give someone compliments as a way to get them to do something?

Lesson 7F—"A Work in Process"

Key Concepts
tween centric of mastery, media depictions of losing
Special Materials/Media
Access to Internet
Intro Questions/Thoughts for Students

- What do you think of these quotes/phrases:

  "A person learns more in defeat than in victory."
  "Winning isn't everything; it's the *only* thing."
  "Second place is the first loser."

- Have you ever had a circumstance where you were proud of losing? Why were you nevertheless proud?

Activity

Have students draw a picture inspired by the prompt "What does 'losing' look like?" Students should then look for movies, TV shows, and ads geared for tweens (ages nine to twelve) that show someone losing at something. They can do this in small groups or as a class, looking for:

- How is losing portrayed, as a really bad thing, as a one-time event, or as a natural part of life (that isn't unusual) for most people?
- Were the losers bad sports, or did they take the loss well?
- Is there any good that comes from the losing? Often the loser comes back to win, but are any other plusses shown with losing (like it was fun just to participate)?
- Do the losers reflect on how or why they lost or take a moment to think about what happened? How do the losers act toward the winners?
- How many stories or ads can you find where the hero (or person you are rooting for) loses at the main quest but feels OK about it?

Follow-up Questions/Discussions

- What positives, if any, did the media you watched depict about losing?
- Are losses depicted more as a single event or as part of a process? If you have participated in a competitive activity for a number of years, have you ever used a loss to better yourself? Is this shown in media?
- Are there other ways to measure success than by being first? Some say there are but they are not as fulfilling or fun. What do you say?

Social Questions for Students

- If you do a personal best in an activity (such as your running time) but don't finish first, how do you feel? What if it's your personal best but you finish last?
- We often compare our lives to others to see if we are "winning," but we don't get the full picture of the other person's life. This is especially true with social media, where life stories are often **curated** (selectively chosen to give a certain impression). Have you ever felt bad because someone else looks like she is "winning" more than you are? What other information may you not be seeing about her life? What "winning" factors about your own life might you be taking for granted?

Lesson 7G—Breaking the Rule Breakers[19]

Key Concepts

tween centric of individuality, rebellion as individuality

Special Materials/Media

Access to Internet, ability to watch clips

Intro Questions/Thoughts for Students

- What does individuality look like? Does it always mean breaking the rules or going against what most people say or do?
- When is it good to break the rules, and when is it good to follow them?
- If someone breaks the rules to be an individual, should he be responsible for both the good and bad that happens from his actions?

Activity

Students should watch shows or movies for examples of when characters decide to be individuals and not do what others are doing. If possible, students should look for instances when characters break a specific rule (such as at school or driving the wrong way). Once a list is generated, students should treat each instance as a mini–court case in which one or two students act as prosecutors arguing that the character should be punished, while one or two others act as defense attorneys trying to have the character not punished or get off with a lighter punishment.[20] The rest of the class acts as the jury who, after hearing both sides, discusses and agrees on a possible punishment. Jobs rotate as each case is addressed.

Follow-up Questions/Discussions

- Was there a pattern to the expressed individuality, such as the character being told not to break the rule and then she does it intentionally, or was the rule breaking more accidental? Does it make a difference in terms of guilt?
- Do the shows generally show positive, negative, or mixed consequences of the rule breaking? If a rule is broken but there is no harm (or even something good results), should there be no punishment?

Social Questions for Students

- Is there a way to conform and still be an individual, or must individuality always be an act of rebellion?

- If you do something you know is against the rules, but you didn't know how much damage or harm it would cause, should you be punished for that harm, for just breaking the rule, or somewhere in between?

Lesson 7H—Change the Story

Key Concepts
tween centric of imagination
Special Materials/Media
old toys like Legos or Barbie dolls (for advanced challenge)
Intro Questions/Thoughts for Students

- Do you ever accept something because "that's the way it's always been"? Have you ever done that with something you didn't like, but it was easier just to go along?
- How might you update something your parents liked as tweens to be popular today?
- When you see or read a retelling of a story, but something is changed from the way you knew it, do you think more often "Hmm, that's interesting" or "That's not right"?

Activity

Students brainstorm traditional stories or fairy tales (from Goldilocks to Spider-Man). They then plan out and present the story, but they must make the ending different to be more "real" or "current" for today's tweens. Other students then discuss whether they like the changed ending better. For an advanced challenge, the students can do this as an improv activity, which can be done in a couple of ways:

- Students plan their story as usual.
- As they come up to perform, the groups are given a random old toy and have two minutes to plan how to incorporate that toy into their skit.
- Additionally, or alternatively, plot elements (slipper doesn't fit, exposed to body-altering gamma rays) are put on index cards. Each group has one random card placed face down in front of their performance. After one minute of performing, the teacher gives a signal for one member of the performing group to read the card. The group must instantly incorporate that new element into their story.

Follow-up Questions/Discussions

- Even though these were well-known stories, was it fun to see the alternatives? If so, why do we sometimes not like it when a story we are used to changes? Is there a comfort to knowing how a story will turn out?
- Many messages to tweens (and children) say to unleash imagination, but how often do you (or kids in general) deviate from the pre-packaged imagination? For example, if you buy a Lego set designed around a space theme, have you ever changed it to take place somewhere else? Could you?
- If imaginary stories can be sold pre-packaged, can ideas also be conveyed this way? Do we just accept when people say, for example, "All _______ are good and all __________ are bad"?

Social Questions for Students

- When is it worth the time and mental effort to try to come up with a better way to do things, and when is it better to just go along for the ride?

Lesson 7I—Cool Pops

Key Concepts
tween centric of popularity, coolness as a tween motivator
Special Materials/Media
Internet for research
Intro Questions/Thoughts for Students

- What does it mean to be popular?
- Is there a general way to act to be popular? Are there certain things one has to do, or look like, to be popular? Do you like that it is this way?
- Is "popular" the same as "cool"? If it helps, make a Venn diagram and list adjectives:

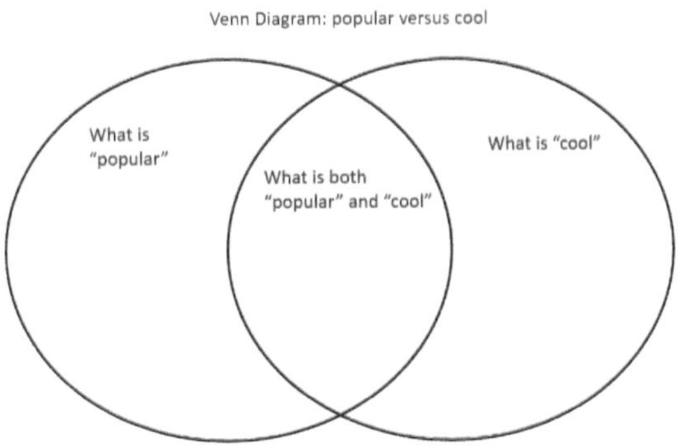

- How has tween "coolness," or what makes a person popular, changed over the years?
- Has your definition of cool or how to be a popular person changed since you were in elementary school? How so? Why?

Activity

Students should be divided into groups, and each group assigned a decade (2010s, 2000s, 1990s, 1980s, 1970s, etc.). Each group is then to be detectives and determine who were tween popular people (either people actually nine to twelve years old or people greatly admired by tweens) in that decade (a great resource for this is the old tween/young teen magazines such as *Tiger Beat*, *Bop*, and *J-14*). As the students analyze the tween-deemed cool people, they should prepare to report back:

- Who were the specific popular tween people? What were they famous for (TV, sports, modeling, or something else)? Ask your parents who was popular in their time, both in their school and nationally.
- Were the popular people also considered "cool"? Were they considered cool by a majority, almost everyone, or just a few (and the rest went along with it)?
- What did popular people wear or do, or how did they look, that seemed to help their popularity back then?
- What was their personality like? Were they happy or edgy? Were they rebellious or nice people (or both)? Were they more an individual or part of a group?[21]
- Based on the tweens you found, what is each decade's definition of a "popular person"?

Once everyone has completed their decade, the groups should add their findings to a class timeline and discuss the changes or similarities over time.

Follow-up Questions/Discussions

- Were there any popular or cool looks or actions of the past you found kind of silly? Do you think people ten years from now will think that about your popular or cool trends now?
- Did you see many scientists or people famous for their knowledge in your historical popular or cool list? Why do you think that is? Do you think that's right?
- How do you think marketers use a tween's desire to be an individual and popular to promote their message or product? Can you find ads that imply you will be a stand-out individual with their product? If everyone does it,

can they all be stand-out individuals? Does someone have to stand out to be cool?
- Many TV shows try to combine coolness and popularity by having a character be a rebel (cool) but admired by everyone (popular). Do you think this can happen in real life? Can a person be on top of the social ladder while trying to cut it down? Why or why not?

Social Questions for Students

- Do you think your definition of who is popular or cool will be the same when you are a teenager? If not, why do we put so much effort into something that doesn't last?
- Is it OK to do things just to be popular or cool? Is that cool? When is it too far?
- Is popularity or coolness at your school based more on outer or inner qualities of a person? Do you like the balance? If not, how could you help change that?

Lesson 7J—Against the Grain

Key Concepts
teen centric of friendship, peer pressure, tacit pressure
Special Materials/Media
Access to TV shows/movies
Intro Questions/Thoughts for Students

- What is "peer pressure"? Why do people give in to it? Would you do something you weren't sure about because a friend or a group of friends asked you to do it? Would it matter if what they asked was to wear a certain product or if it was to be mean to a person one of your friends didn't like?
- Does peer pressure have to be exerted by directly telling someone they should do something? Can peer pressure be exerted by everyone doing something, which makes the one not doing it feel they should (**tacit pressure**[22])? There is an old expression: "When in Rome, do as the Romans do." What do you think that means?
- When can peer pressure be a good thing, and when can it be a bad thing?

Activity

Discuss with students the concept of peer pressure. They should understand that it is not just overt pressure ("Hey, why aren't you doing this like everyone else?"), but it is often exerted by **tacit pressure** where a person feels the need to conform to what a majority of people are doing (like getting quiet in a room where everyone else is). Tacit pressure can also be exerted by **influencers**, or people with social power, such as a teacher in a class.

Afterward, students should watch tween shows or movies for incidents of peer pressure:

Show	Describe scene	Overt or tacit pressure?	Pressure by group or influencer?	Result? Good or bad result of decision?

Results can be tabulated and discussed.

After discussion, students should look for peer pressure messages around school, filling out another chart as above but in real life. They should also look for advertising that uses peer pressure by conveying that all tweens are doing something/wearing something/buying something,[23] or that friendship somehow means buying their products.

Follow-up Questions/Discussions

- How does the way peer pressure is depicted in shows match what you see in real life? How does it differ?
- Tacit pressure is very hard to see because it is just accepted as the norm and taken for granted (like boys wearing pants). Often it takes an outsider to point it out ("We don't celebrate that holiday"). Can you think of something you might have missed?
- Were the results of giving in to peer pressure, at least the overt kind, generally good, bad, or mixed? Was there an overt message about peer pressure in the show? Were the people yielding to peer pressure glad they did or remorseful?
- Were there any cases of "double pressure," where one group of peers said to do one thing, but another said to do something else? How was it resolved?

Social Questions for Students

- Do you feel peer pressure in your life to do things, both things you want to do and things you do not want to do? Do you relate to any particular character or situation you saw in a show? Can you use how it turned out in that show to help you?
- What do you think of the phrase, "If you were really my friend, you would (or would not) do it?" When is using that phrase OK, and when is it not?

- If a friend were to say that you are doing something bad or that puts people off (like the jokes you tell hurt feelings or that you talk too loudly), but he is trying to help you for your sake, how would you take it?

Lesson 7K—Sore Winner

Key Concepts
tween centric of superiority
Special Materials/Media
camera, ability to show film clips and survey
Intro Questions/Thoughts for Students

- Is it better to be a good loser or a bad winner?
- How do we find the right balance between celebrating our victories and not making the other contestants feel bad, whether it's grades, sports, or getting something good (like a great family trip)?

Activity

Students should talk about four categories of people in competitions in terms of attitude after the competition:

- good winners
- bad winners
- good losers
- bad losers

The students can brainstorm ideas about what each looks like. Then they should try to brainstorm movie or TV show clips of each. For fun, the students can also make their own movie with the students as writers, actors, directors, and editors. Once the clips are assembled, students can survey others by asking people to watch the clips and rank the four types of people by whom they admire, with 4 being the person they admire most and 1 the least. Students can also ask *why* respondents did or did not admire the people and any personal data students want to analyze, such as gender, age, or whether the respondent has done the activities shown (like racing).[24]

Follow-up Questions/Discussions

- One tricky part of conducting surveys is controlling *variables*, or factors that might change or skew the data if they differ between respondents. Asking people who are just one kind of person (athletes, children) might skew the data so it doesn't represent people at large. Why do you think it was important to mix up the order of the video clips shown?

- Even if one part of your data is pretty fixed (people admire the good winner most, the bad loser least), it is the middle that often reveals the most interesting findings. What did you find?
- Did people identify any particular behaviors that they liked or not? Was it more the bad loser's/winner's attitude or their words and actions?

Social Questions for Students

- It's hard not to have a positive attitude in winning or a negative one when losing, but how can we make sure our words and actions are not too extreme in that circumstance?
- How might you react in real life to a bad loser or bad winner? What would you do if someone told *you* that you were being a bad loser or bad winner?

Lesson 7L—Cen-tricks of the Trade

Key Concepts

tween centrics as influencers

Special Materials/Media

miscellaneous art supplies for a mock device (boxes, paper towel rolls, tape, markers, etc.)

Intro Questions/Thoughts for Students

- What is a minor but chronic (repeating) problem that you have, either at home (having trouble waking up, having to walk the dog) or at school (heavy backpack, don't like lunch food)? What kind of magical device would fix it? How could you get other tweens to buy it?

Activity

Students in pairs or threes interview each other about a chronic problem. Together, they invent a device that would solve their problems. They should then build a mockup of their invention with art supplies and create a thirty-second ad that not only shows the problem/solution but also uses one of the seven tween centrics as a persuasion device. If the group does ads for both (or all) inventions, each must use a different tween centric. Alternatively, the teacher can assign a tween centric to each group.

As each group presents their ad or ads, the rest of the class tries to figure out which tween centric(s) is (are) being used, identifying the clues that led them to that deduction.

Follow-up Questions/Discussions

- Were some centrics easier to match up with some inventions than others? Why?
- Can the centrics be used for non-goods, like ideas of school loyalty, don't do drugs, or don't cheat? Try to make a PSA (public service announcement) using the centrics.

Social Questions for Students

- Have you ever had someone try to convince you of something, but they put you off because they were trying too hard? What did you do? What could you say to them?
- Have you ever been told you were trying too hard to speak or look a certain way? How did you react?
- When is it better to be direct, even obvious, when delivering a message, and when is it better to be indirect or subtle?

Lesson 7M—Teen Romance

Key Concepts
tween **aspirational thinking** of teen life
Special Materials/Media
teens to interview
Intro Questions/Thoughts for Students

- What do you think life will be like when you are a teenager? What will be the same? What will be different? Better or worse? In what ways?
- How do tweens who don't have older siblings get their ideas about what the next stage, teen life, will be like? How accurate do you think it is?

Activity

Students should brainstorm movies and TV shows that depict teen life. They should then watch them as if these were the only source of information as to what teen life is like regarding:

- What percentage of a teen's life is devoted to school, being at home, hanging with friends, etc.?
- What are the main concerns of teens?
- What are the main activities of teens (studying, dating, etc.)?

Now, equipped with this data, students should conduct personal interviews with teens, asking them about their percentage of time actually spent on the various activities and what their main concerns are. The students can even show some of the clips to the teens and ask how accurate the teen feels the representation is. Students should also ask what the biggest surprises of teen years were (what they didn't know about as tweens).

Follow-up Questions/Discussions

- How much did the real teens say media glamorizes teen life? What areas were the most accurate? What areas were the most glamorized?
- Based on the real teen interviews, do you think tweens are well informed about going into teen years? What is something you wish media showed more about teen years, either as entertainment or so tweens would have a better idea? If you have some suggestions, write to the companies that produce these shows.

Social Questions for Students

- Are you looking forward to your teen years or are you worried? What things make you look forward to your teen years and what give you concern or worry? For things about teen years that concern you, what can you do now to better help you for when you are a teen? Do you think other people your age have the same concerns?
- As wise old tweens, what did you not know as a child about tween years that you wish you had known? Write a letter to elementary-school teachers to let them know facets of tween years that should be addressed to elementary school kids or offer to make a presentation to elementary kids on how to better succeed as a middle schooler.

Lesson 7N—Adult or a Dolt?

Key Concepts
adult representation in tween media
Special Materials/Media
access to tween shows
Intro Questions/Thoughts for Students

- How much do you think parents, your teachers, and other adults are aware of what is going on in your life? Roughly, about what percentage of your life do such adults currently know about? Who knows the most?

- Do you think the adults in your world know about being a tween today, or are they ignorant about some things? What areas do adults know about, and what areas are they ignorant of?
- Do you think tween-oriented TV shows and movies accurately portray adult supervision and interaction with tweens?

Activity

Students should list the most popular shows for tweens that are centered on tween life (a Marvel superhero movie, while popular with tweens, would not count, as the central characters are not tweens). For such shows, students are to observe the depictions of the adults who are key to the tween characters and how the tweens and adults interact. Specific note should be taken of:

- How much of the tween's life is independent of adults?
- How often are the adults fooled or tricked by the tweens?
- Who are the most knowledgeable about that tween's life: parents, teachers, or a third adult? Is there an issue that the adult educates the tween about? Is there a topic that the tween educates the adult about? Is it about a tween issue (school) or an adult issue (monster threatening the world)?

Follow-up Questions/Discussions

- On the one hand, tween shows empower tweens to feel independent of adults. On the other hand, were there any scenes that you felt went too far? When should shows encourage tweens to solve problems for themselves, and when should tween shows portray tweens seeking adult guidance?
- Many say, "It's just a show," but do you think the portrayals of adults can have an impact on how tweens see them?[25]
- How much are either the tweens or the adults willing to learn from each other (even if reluctantly)? Does this reflect your experiences?

Social Questions for Students

- Who are your go-to adults for different concerns or advice?
- What kind of problems should you notify an adult about, and what things can wait?
- When adults tell you about when they were tweens, do you find it helpful?
- What areas or issues of tween life are the same as when your parents were your age, and what areas or issues are different?

Lesson 7O—Gnothi Seauton

Key Concepts

teen self-awareness in message processing

Special Materials/Media

None

Intro Questions/Thoughts for Students

- The phrase *gnothi seauton* is from ancient Greek and means "know thyself." It was written at the Temple of Apollo at Delphi and, even more famously, was a cornerstone of the teachings of the famous teacher and philosopher Socrates. What do you think it means to "know thyself"? Why is it considered such a deep and challenging command? Two thousand years after Socrates, Ice Cube rapped that you should "check yo'self before you wreck yo'self." Is he saying the same thing? Do any other songs say the same thing?
- How does "know thyself" apply to a group, such as a class? What can be learned from seeing a whole group's response if you are a member of that group?
- Sometimes indirect clues tell you about people, or even yourself, such as seeing someone fidgeting can tell you he is nervous. What do you think a person's shopping habits can reveal about the way he thinks about himself or the world around him?

Activity

Have students take the following survey anonymously.

CONSUMERISM COMMUNITY SURVEY

(*Know thyself*—Socrates)

Please answer each question by your gut instinct. Please do not change your answer or go back to a previous question. DO NOT PUT YOUR NAME ON THIS!!!!!

Part 1—The Ratings Game:

For each question, please indicate where you are on the number grid as follows:

(not very much) 1 . . . 2 . . . 3 . . . 4 . . . 5 (extremely)

1. How savvy (ability to make good judgments) of a shopper do you consider yourself?
2. How much do name brands affect your shopping choices in general?
3. For each of the following product types, indicate how much brand names affect your choice of which product to buy:

    - Restaurants/Food:
    - Clothes:
    - Electronics:

4. How likely would you be to buy a generic or knock-off brand of shoes of the same quality as a name brand if no one were to know?
5. How likely would you be to buy a generic or knock-off brand of shoes of the same quality as a name brand if your friends would KNOW that the product is generic/knock-off?
6. If you become aware that a particular company gives to charity or does community service, to what extent does this make you more likely to purchase their product over a competitor's?

Part 2—Who are You?

Please give a short answer to each:

1. What do you consider to be "cool" brands?
2. Considering your personality, if you were a soft drink, what would it be (not what you like to drink)? Please feel free to say why.
3. At about what age today do people in your community stop being a "kid" and start being a young adult?
4. "Everybody" will be at a really big outdoor party you are going to attend, and so you go shopping for new sunglasses. For the product attributes below, please rank them from most (1) to least (6) important in your buying decision:

The glasses are:

The most popular style: _____

Very effective against UV rays: _____

Inexpensive: _____

A very hot brand in Hollywood and you would be the first to have them in your town: ______

Very unique and one of a kind: _____

Long-lasting/durable: _____

The collective results should be tabulated. Subgroups of students should be tasked with determining the best way to display the data (graph, pie chart, written out) to explain to others.

Follow-up Questions/Discussions

- What categories had clear class preferences and what categories had the least?
- Why do you think the survey asks you about brand names? Do you think there is a difference between people who shop and care about brand names and those who don't? Importantly, what might also account for why some people consider name brands and some don't?[26]
- In general, do you like taking surveys about yourself? Why or why not? What are your favorite kinds? Can you learn anything from them?

Social Questions for Students

- Were your answers more with the majority or with the minority? How did that make you feel? Do you have a preference for having the same opinion as the group or not? What kinds of opinions do you like sharing with the majority, and what kind do you like being different or in the minority?
- Have you ever reconsidered your opinion because a majority disagreed with it? When should you consider doing that, and when should you not?

NOTES

1. For a discussion of augmented reality, see Jim Wasserman and David Loveland, "More than Reality," *American School Board Journal* 204, no. 2 (April 2017), which we are gratuitously promoting here.
2. If you recognize that reference, you were an early adopter of computer games from the late 1970s and early 1980s!
3. David Siegel, Timothy Coffey, and Gregory Livingston, *The Great Tween Buying Machine: Marketing to Today's Tweens* (Ithaca, NY: Paramount Market Publishing, 2001).
4. Siegel et al., *Great Tween Buying Machine*, 3.
5. We'll just call all three "Siegel" to save time here, with the promise that if they ever all come for dinner, we will address each one individually.
6. Siegel et al., *Great Tween Buying Machine*, 9.
7. Like Harry Potter, the superhero metamorphosis story may be intentionally or unintentionally evocative of puberty, resonating with tweens.
8. Siegel et al., *Great Tween Buying Machine*, 43–49.
9. One of us did have a circumstance in class where a student, who usually remained quiet with an air of removed indifference, once threw up her hand and said, "Aren't you doing the very thing you are warning us about? I mean, by your seeming to be on our side fighting off marketing that falsely says, 'We're on your side,' you're making us more receptive to *your* message of being media literate!" If she said not another word, she earned her A.
10. Siegel et al., *Great Tween Buying Machine*, 50.
11. Speaking of stepping into the same river twice, "coolness" as a persuasive tool is particularly explored in chapter 4.

12. As far back as the seventeenth century, philosopher John Locke explored the existence of truly imaginary thinking, though he contended that there were no innate ideas and that imaginative concepts like a *unicorn* were really the reassembling of experienced things like a horse plus a horn. Feel free to stop and discuss, but such fantasy-popping theories are why John Locke's treatises were never popular with children.

13. Some parents have experienced this when their child cannot find the Lego piece indicated in the next step or seen the child's horrified reaction to "You don't have to build it that way; you can do it any way you want."

14. Go ahead, look it up on YouTube; we'll wait.

15. Massive Multiplayer Online Role-Playing Game, such as *World of Warcraft*.

16. See, for example, Holly K. M. Henry and Dina L. G. Borzekowski, "The Nag Factor: How Do Children Convince Their Parents to Buy Unhealthy Foods?" Johns Hopkins University Bloomberg School of Public Health, August 11, 2011, https://www.jhsph.edu/news/news-releases/2011/borzekowski-nag-factor.html. It's also referred to as "pester power."

17. Because teens are so preoccupied with where they stand in relation to this brave new world they have migrated to, they tend to be highly responsive to self-surveys and opportunities to see what "type" they are.

18. See Siegel et al., *Great Tween Buying Machine*, 45–49. There is a satisfying sense of irony in using the very type of experiment marketers use to infiltrate tweens' minds in order to reinforce their media literacy defenses!

19. While this is similar to lesson 4F, it is different in that the focus is more to get tweens to weigh the depiction of rebellion versus its real-life consequences.

20. This exercise can also be done as a fishbowl.

21. See chapter 3 and lesson 3C regarding **persona**.

22. See lesson 6D for an investigation of tacit pressure as regards children. Here, the tacit pressure is applied less by society than by peers, which is more a tween circumstance.

23. See lesson 4C on the **bandwagon effect**.

24. As a reminder, surveyors need to be unbiased and try not to say, "This is a good winner" or anything else that might give the survey away or nudge the respondents. It would also help if surveyors showed the clips in different orders so that one clip doesn't always follow another.

25. See chapter 3 on the stalagmite effect.

26. Something that you are not looking for or even mindful of that affects results is called an **extraneous variable**. We discussed in chapter 1 that experiments and surveys in this book are more for gaining exposure to social sciences than precisely controlling data, but how might extraneous variables be better controlled here?

Chapter Eight

Media Literacy, Relativity, and Persuasion

There is an old joke (which usually means it's no longer funny) in Boy Scouting:

> *Question: How do you tell a Boy Scout?*
> *Answer: In a calm, soothing voice so as not to startle the Boy Scout before telling him what you want to say!*

Slightly more profound (though certainly not as grandpa-knee-slappingly humorous), philosopher and early pioneer of media literacy Marshall McLuhan famously said that "the medium is the message," meaning that the way a message was conveyed was just as important and had just as much an effect on listeners as the content of the message itself. In both the joke and McLuhan's statement, the idea is that the modality of how a message is conveyed is as much a part of the persuasion as the merits of the message itself.

We think of ourselves as stationary, catching messages as they come to us and then deciding for ourselves if the message has merit and therefore should be embraced. In economics, this idea is often summed up by the notion of **consumer sovereignty**, that the consumer of goods (or information)[1] has the last and ultimate control of what is produced or is successful in the market. In both cases, however, it is a question of relativity; the consumer may think he is stationary, but he has been actually brought closer to the message by the message's delivery techniques, so that he is quicker to take it in and more receptive to inculcating the core message into his belief system.

Whether one puts this relativism in terms of media literacy, Einsteinian metaphors about two moving trains, or even Michel de Montaigne's sixteenth-century question, "When I am playing with my cat, how do I know she is not playing with me?" consumers of information need to be aware of how they are being primed for the message, as well as how the message is being primed for them.

As explored previously in chapter 7, the young teen mind is awash in hormones that trigger the amygdala to hop in the driver's seat and take our decision making for a ride, at least until about age twenty-five when the prefrontal cortex gets a safety brake with which to slow down the emotional reckless driving. That does not mean, however, that emotion has no persuasive ability before the teen years or is completely neutralized afterward.

Empathy develops at a very young age, as young as two years old, and while it remains a valuable window through which we can see, understand, and connect with others, that window is also a portal into our own psyches, employed by those who would nudge us to respond favorably to their own messaging ends by using humor, love, and other emotional touchpoints to make us more receptive to the message before it is even heard.[2]

Ivan Pavlov was the famous Russian researcher who showed that if something neutral, like ringing a bell, was activated at the same time as something good—feeding his dogs—the dogs came to link the two and have positive reactions to the bell alone, salivating in anticipation when they heard the ringing of the bell. Can such **conditioning** also happen with ads, where one's positive feelings toward an entertaining ad, over time, become linked to the product itself?

In a less direct method, sometimes bringers of bad news soften up the information receiver by first delivering good news or amusing them or by laying out a general persuasive argument so that the receiver is in a more congenial or receptive mood before the unwelcomed bit comes at the end. Even Thomas Jefferson laid out his arguments first, from general to more specific, and only actually declared America's independence in the last paragraph of his famous break-up letter to King George.

See Lesson 8A—Emotion Promotion in Motion

Even as we arrive at the spot to receive the information and perhaps points of view of the messengers, we arrive with baggage in hand, that baggage being our own biases that become more entrenched when confirmed but resistant if challenged or countered. Interestingly, the word **stereotype** comes from the idea of mass printing, where a plate is used to print the same thing over and over again (like a picture reproduction).

See Lesson 8B—Martian Chronicles

See Lesson 8C—It's an Ad, Ad, Ad, Ad World!

Once we've come into contact with the message, we look for a path to follow from it: how should we carry on with the new information just handed to us? Do we believe it? Do we weigh the message with rational thinking or gut feeling? We are supposed to go somewhere or do something because of the message, but where and what? Like many new arrivals, we look for signs, and information peddlers are more than happy to point the way. Contained in the messages are **focus nudges** to guide us, but that can make us only consider what the messengers point to rather than seeing all the sights. This creates a potential problem of our being focus-nudged into assumptions, presumptions, and overgeneralizations, especially when the messenger, knowingly or unknowingly, curates the message to give an imbalanced overview or **slant**, coupled with our own biases that lead us to follow certain trails of thought over others.[3]

One of us does a quick demonstration for classes by standing at the front of the room and asking students to intensely focus on his finger that is held up. After thirty seconds, the teacher asks the class if, while they looked at his finger, they saw the second hand of the clock ticking away about three feet above the finger. Most of the class will say they did not, but the teacher then reminds them that the laws of physics did not change; light continued to refract off the second hand and into their eyes, but the students' brains just chose to ignore those light signals because the teacher instructed them to! In media terms, we see this in broadcasts that provide summation (like thirty-minute news programs) or "headline" news; we focus on the "top stories" because we are told they are the top stories, even if one station's top story is a potential war on the other side of the world while another's is about a local boy trapped in a well.

See Lesson 8D—What's News with You?

See Lesson 8E—Triangulating Truth

See Lesson 8F—Seeing in Two Dimensions

Whether a message is skewed intentionally or unintentionally, message receivers need to be aware of such nudges so that they can counter-steer or at least be aware that their attention is being pulled a certain way by the words, pictures, and other stimuli that accompany the message. To be clear, there really is no such thing as an unbiased, non-slanted message. There are so many facts regarding any particular issue that as soon as a messenger decides fact A is worth relaying in detail, fact B should be summarized, or fact C should be left out, they have curated the transferal of information and opened the door to possible inaccuracies, mis-depictions, and misunderstanding.

A **fallacy** is when a person makes an argument or conclusion based on faulty facts or reasoning. A common one is a **hasty generalization**,[4] where a person assumes everyone or everything in a group is like a very small sample. As long as we are on guard and look for such pitfalls, however, we are still the better for being exposed to and exchanging divergent information and perspectives. It's like human interaction: mixing with people increases your risk of catching a cold, but as long as we take precautions, life is better shared with others than alone in an antiseptic cell.

See Lesson 8G—Mountain of Information

See Lesson 8H—Is That Spelled with I or U?

See Lesson 8I—Aligning Words and Actions

See Lesson 8J—Indirection

If one or two well-placed words can nudge us into thinking a certain way, imagine what pictures can do, given that they are purportedly worth one thousand words (and that's for simple pictures at the old exchange rates). Because we rarely consciously say, "Look at that," but instead take in most visuals passively, it's important to first check whether our visual receiver has any pre-set filters, or if the signals are automatically assigned meaning as we decode. Even what's not center to our viewing but merely "background" can add meaning to our perspective.

See Lesson 8K—Feeling in the Pink, or Are You Blue?

See Lesson 8L—Text vs. Context

See Lesson 8M—Stranger in a Strange Land

When we see two things side by side, we can't help but compare and contrast them. This is called **juxtaposition**, and it can be done verbally ("Whereas . . . ") or pictorially with "before" and "after" pictures. When a messenger sets up a picture (or anything in it, such as colors) to make you think a certain way, this is called **implied messaging**. It persuades us through our "gut" (**visceral**) response rather than our mental (**rational**) processing.

Even being aware of our own visual presumptions is not enough, as we then have to consider how the messenger's presumptions and visual interpretations seep into our own seemingly internal, independent valuation. Search engines like Google use algorithms, complex sets of coded rules, to decide what you most likely want in your latest Internet search based on what you, and other people it thinks are like you (location, age, etc.), have looked at or searched for before.

***See* Lesson 8N—Can You See the Real Me, Can Ya?**

***See* Lesson 8O—Alphabetically, *After* Comes Before *Before* . . . Weird, Huh?**

***See* Lesson 8P—Drawn In**

Finally, while we are predisposed to first and perhaps primarily take in the world by our eyes, our ears are likewise taking in the world (and never getting a break at night, like our eyes do). Maybe because they're on the sides of our head and we don't think about them (until cold weather hits) but ancient media as far back as radio have been masters at giving us sounds and letting us draw the accompanying pictorial conclusions.

***See* Lesson 8Q—Oh, What a Knight!**

***See* Lesson 8R—Noisy Theater of the Mind**

CHAPTER 8 ACCOMPANYING LESSONS

Lesson 8A—Emotion Promotion in Motion

Key Concepts
emotional influence and emotional manipulation in messaging
Special Materials/Media
Access to ads
Intro Questions/Thoughts for Students

- Have you ever told a story but saved the most important part, like whom you were talking about, until the end? Why do you (and others) tell stories that way?
- When you want to convince your parents of something, do you sometimes "lay the groundwork" to get them more receptive before you ask?
- Do you find people are more open to messages if they are first put in a good mood, are laughing, or are sympathetic?

Activity

Students are to look for ads where the product or brand is not directly identified until the end. They should analyze the ad for the following:

- What mood is the ad trying to put you in before they reveal who they are?
- Are there hints before the reveal, such as glimpses of the product or brand? Once you know the brand, is it easier to see the clues beforehand?
- How is the brand reveal done? Is it dramatic or more "Oh, by the way, it's us"?

Students can present their ads and ask others to watch and see how long before they know the product and brand.

Follow-up Questions/Discussions

- Why do you think some marketers wait to tell you who they are? Is it that you are drawn into a "story" more than a direct sales pitch? Is it for the mystery or to first get you in a receptive mood to then sell to you?
- Can ads that give you positive feelings, over time, become linked to the product itself, like Pavlov's dogs?
- Even if you don't particularly like the product, do you think the fact that an ad is emotionally engaging makes you remember the brand or even convinces you to buy?

Social Questions for Students

- What is the difference between making someone more "receptive" to your message and taking advantage of their emotions?
- If a person in authority wants you to do something, do they ever first get you sympathetic to a problem, then tell you what they want you to do? Remembering the Declaration of Independence, does the "move first, then self-identify" strategy work with nonmarketing messages?

Lesson 8B—Martian Chronicles

Key Concepts

stereotypes in media, **feedback loop** (self-validation) of expectation and behavior, **confirmation bias**

Special Materials/Media

Access to media

Intro Questions/Thoughts for Students

- How much of what we think about others is based not on firsthand experience but on media images? When media portray particular groups, do they show a wide variety of possibilities, or do they tend to show a few certain stereotypes? How can we tell when we are seeing a **stereotype**?
- Once you have an idea about something, do you generally assume all such things are like that? What is an example of a thing or place you tried once and then assumed it was always like that, such as a restaurant?
- Have you ever assumed someone likes or doesn't like something, or does or does not do an activity, based on how they look (like assuming a tall person plays basketball)?

Activity

You are a Martian sent as a spy to investigate and report back on Earth (and particularly American) culture. You know nothing of Earth, but figure you can learn about Earthlings' ways by monitoring their media.

Watch various media, and look for general observations to report back to your leader about different groups, such as:

- women, especially those with particular features (such as blondes or wearing glasses);
- people from particular regions (such as the Middle East);
- people from particular areas of the United States (such as the South or Hollywood);
- people of particular ages, races, socioeconomic status, or roles (such as parents); or
- activities, such as high school classes or spring break.

Remember, you know nothing beforehand, so everything you learn about this group/activity is from its general portrayal in media. A human wearing sunglasses inside might indicate humans are very light sensitive (which must be typical because no one is telling him not to do so).

Follow-up Questions/Discussions

- You already know something about most of the types of people you saw, so you can often tell when a person is not a good representative of a group. But what about types of people you don't know a lot about? Do you think you might have a skewed view of them like the Martian would?
- When you hear of something "everyone is doing," have you ever then joined in, which ultimately confirms the original statement (which may or may not have been true at the time)? This is called a **feedback loop**. What are the positives and negatives of such a phenomenon?

- If our primary source for knowing about people is based on stereotypes, we then think of that stereotype and look to confirm it, reinforcing our belief (and labeling those that don't fit the stereotype as "weird" or "abnormal"). Might groups depicted stereotypically see that as a message of what they "should" be like and possibly imitate it?

Social Questions for Students

- What things do people assume about you because you identify as belonging to a certain group? What might be a stereotype you assume about other groups?
- Have you ever acted a certain way or expressed an opinion more because people expected you to than you really wanted to?

Lesson 8C—It's an Ad, Ad, Ad, Ad World!

Key Concepts

tailoring ads to reflect local culture, getting the perspective of a different culture

Special Materials/Media

Access to international ads (YouTube is good for this)

Intro Questions/Thoughts for Students

- We have explored how ads are tailored to different groups in the United States,[5] but do persuaders make different arguments and pitches in every country? Do people see the same product differently in other countries? What can ads tell us about other cultures?
- Do you know of any customs or practices you do that would be seen as odd in other countries?

Activity

Look at ads for Coca-Cola, Pepsi, or other international brands in different countries. Make a list of ways the ads are similar to American ads and ways they are different, even though it is the same product. Look for things such as:

- the way different people (men and women, older and younger) interact;
- the similarities and differences of a situation (school classroom, on a date) that also happen in the United States; and
- the way humor, jokes, or something funny is expressed. Would it also be funny in the United States?

Follow-up Questions/Discussions

- As a class, discuss what experiences seem to be universal (family, courtship, school) and what seem to not be. Based on the ads, do you think people share common experiences across cultures, or are there fundamental differences in cultural values?
- If people living in other countries only knew about American culture from our ads (say, for Coke and Pepsi), what might they conclude?[6]
- Beyond ads, do individuals change their argument or message to convince people of different backgrounds?

Social Questions for Students

- Do you ever change how you dress or act, or what you say, to fit in with different crowds or circumstances? Is that OK, or is it being a "poser"? What about changing your ethics or values? What if you want to fit in, but the way a group does something doesn't seem right to you (like ignoring or being mean to certain people)?
- How much is it OK to borrow from or imitate other people's dress, way of talking, or culture? Does it depend on your intent in imitating?

Lesson 8D—What's News with You?

Key Concepts

accuracy of television news, **slant** by time allocation

Special Materials/Media

Access to time-limited news programs (TV, radio, or Internet)

Intro Questions/Thoughts for Students

- We seem to live in a world with infinite sources of news, but do they differ in what they cover?
- Summation news (like thirty-minute news programs) are a great way to see the top stories, but how does each news source choose which are the "top stories"? How do they decide how much time to spend not only on news stories but on other areas of life (sports, weather)?
- Do you think the time someone (such as a news outlet) spends on a story reflects how important it is? Conversely, if a news medium does not cover a story, does that make you feel it is less important?
- When an all-news channel such as CNN or Fox devotes many hours to a story, does that imply it is important? Who decides how important a news story is, the broadcaster or the listener?

Activity

Have students watch a thirty-minute news program and then write down the news stories in order and time spent. Have them also write a quick general impression of the story. Compare that with other students who watched a different station or broadcast. Did they cover the same stories in the same order? Did the programs spend about the same amount of time on the same story? Was there a different perceived angle or bias (**slant**) to the story on different stations?

As a fun follow-up activity, have small groups of students summarize famous fairy tales or stories in no more than two minutes. The audience listens and takes notes so that they can compare for parts of the fairy tale included and parts left out.

As a second follow-up, have students get a daily newspaper or go to a news website. In a group, they are to assume the role of TV news director. Students decide which four or five news stories and three or four sports stories to put in their broadcast. Given about twenty minutes (to make time for the weather), can they cover ten news/sports stories accurately? What about if it was a broadcast of school news and events?

Follow-up Questions/Discussions

- Do you think news sources give more time to more important stories, more complicated ones (that need more explanation), ones more interesting to the public, or the ones they like?
- On the other side, should all-news media limit the time they spend on a particular story? What impression do viewers get of a story covered all day?
- How can time-limited newscasts do a better job? Write a letter to let them know.

Social Questions for Students

- When you summarize your day to your parents or friends, do you focus more on what was important, what was different and interesting, or what was typical?
- When you say you have an "open mind" about an issue or person, how honestly "open" is it? For what kinds of issues do you already have a good idea of which side you are on?

Lesson 8E—Triangulating Truth

Key Concepts

partisanship/slant in choosing facts to report, need for personal research

Special Materials/Media

Access to Internet

Intro Questions/Thoughts for Students

- Have you ever been told about something and had a strong reaction to it, but then found out there was another side or more facts that changed your opinion?
- When a big news event happens, do we get enough facts from just one source? How do we receive information yet remain an active participant in understanding news events?

Activity

Have students brainstorm aloud major recent news events they have heard about (attack, election, big game, etc.). Divide the class up and have one part read sources from one side exclusively (conservative, foreign journals, etc.) and the other part from the "opposite" side (liberal, American journals, etc.). Have both groups then publicly fill in two sides of a triangle:

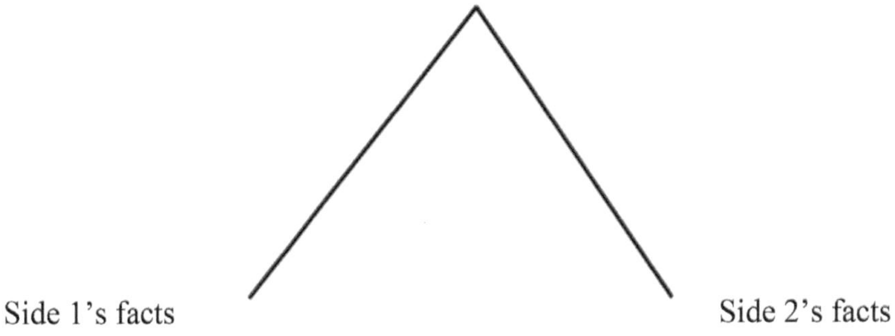

Students should then discuss:

- What facts are in agreement?
- What facts are in dispute?
- What *other* facts would you like to know?

Students then do further research to complete the triangle with missing facts.

Follow-up Questions/Discussions

- Were more facts from the two sides in agreement or disputed?

- Was there a difference as to the type of facts agreed upon versus the disputed facts?
- Do you think the omission of facts is intentional to slant the story or because of other reasons not necessarily intended to persuade (such as limited space or cost)?
- Research how many people say they get their news principally from one source. How informed do you think they are?

Social Questions for Students

- How often do you hear one side of a story (say, an argument between friends) and decide before hearing other views? Even when you hear the other views, have you already partially decided ("First to speak is first to be believed")?
- It's hard to gather all the various parts of an incident or story. Is there anything you and your peers can do when such an incident occurs to get the full story before deciding?

Lesson 8F—Seeing in Two Dimensions

Key Concepts
argumentation, fact vs. opinion (**editorial**) in news
Special Materials/Media
newspaper or printable online news source, two colors of highlighter
Intro Questions/Thoughts for Students

- What is the difference between a fact and an opinion? When people say they are "just giving us the facts," are they always? Can you tell when an opinion is portrayed as a fact?
- What is an editorial? Why are they usually separated from news articles?

Activity

Students should locate the op-ed page of a newspaper and read editorials (or columns by professionals on news sites). Break down the writer's claims by highlighting the *facts* he or she uses in one color and his or her *opinions* in another color. Compare to other students' evaluations of the same piece. If one student marked something as a fact and another student marked it as opinion, discuss why each student thought that.

As follow-up, students should find an editorial that gives an opinion on the same issue but from the other side and do the same thing. Finally, circle any facts mentioned in one piece but not the other.

Follow-up Questions/Discussions

- How much of the editorials was fact versus opinion? Were there any "disguised opinions," such as saying "everyone knows . . . " when there is in fact a disagreement?
- If each is using facts the other doesn't, can we get a clear picture by one source? Can you have "your facts" and "my facts" ("subjective facts"), or must all facts be considered by everyone for a thorough analysis?
- Were there any contradictory facts? How can we resolve this?
- Would a third opinion help? Why or why not?
- What is the danger of thinking an opinion is a fact?

Social Questions for Students

- We sometimes see the world as black or white, as "you either agree and are with me or disagree and are against me." When is this true/false way of looking at things helpful, and when is it counterproductive?
- Is compromise "selling out"? When can it be OK, and when is it important to stand firm?
- Read some of the comments below online editorials. Do the ones that insult the writer influence your perspective on the editorial?
- Do you think worse of the person insulted or the one making the insult?

Lesson 8G—Mountain of Information

Key Concepts
labels affecting perception, **confirmation bias**
Special Materials/Media
picture of a mountain
Intro Questions/Thoughts for Students

- Have you ever thought that something or someone was a certain way, only to find out later it was different (or seen differently by other people)?
- Are there things you haven't yet tried that you already know you would or would not like? How do you know that? Are there people you have never met but you hear they are nice or mean (like the teachers you will have next year)?
- What is a **preconception**?

Activity

The class is divided into four groups. Each is shown (secretly) the same picture of a mountain, but each group's picture has a different caption:

- Mountain of Doom
- Sugar Sweet Mountain
- Mountain of Peace
- Adventure Mountain

Each group then makes up a story about the mountain and an event that happens on it, including adjectives that describe the mountain and how it looks. Bonus if they can come up with music that would be played in the background to the picture!

Reveal the picture and ask: which group had this picture? Read the different stories aloud.

Follow-up Questions/Discussions

- How do the stories and adjectives about the mountain differ? Does the mountain look different as you hear the different stories? Is it hard to see the mountain in a new way?
- As a follow-up activity, look for a photo with a caption that can sway someone's opinion before they even read the article. Look at the title of something or someone, such as a principal or doctor, and discuss how you feel or what you presume about them just by their title.

Social Questions for Students

- Do you ever judge other students by what you are told about them before actually getting to know them? What are the first images you get when told to think of a kid who is a "jock," a "social person," or a "religious person"?
- Can you think of a situation where you began by having one perception but then it changed? Why did you have that first perception, and why did it change?

Lesson 8H—Is That Spelled with I or U?

Key Concepts

use of **first person** vs. **second person** in persuasion

Special Materials/Media

Access to ads

Intro Questions/Thoughts for Students

- Have you ever had to give advice or constructive feedback to someone? How did you do it to be effective but not hurt people's feelings?
- To help soften feedback, have you ever chosen to be indirect, such as saying, "*I* wouldn't have done that" rather than "*You* shouldn't have done that"? Why did you phrase it the way you did? On the other hand, have you ever chosen to be direct with advice, such as saying, "You would look great in that" rather than "I, or anyone else, would look great in that"? When is each technique best? Does one work better with a certain kind of problem/product than another?

Activity

Have students collect ads that have "I" (or "my") and "you" (or "your") statements. Have students try to look specifically for health/medical/beauty ads. Once collected, students should try to form a general rule of advertising or messaging ("use 'I' when you want to persuade someone to . . . , use 'you' when you want someone to . . . ").

As a follow-up, students should think of messages they might want to say to people (don't pollute, be nice to each other, do your homework, etc.). They should then in groups decide whether an "I" or "you" statement would be a better persuader and come up with a poster ad to broadcast the message.

Follow-up Questions/Discussions

- What patterns did you find in the use of "I" versus "you" statements? Are "I" statements used more for medical conditions ("I relieved my itching") and "you" more for aesthetic circumstances ("You'll look great")? Why is that? How do we as a society decide which problems are medical and which cosmetic? How do they overlap? If someone is depressed over how they look, which is it?
- If the "I" ad had used "you," how would it change the tone of the ad? Would it make a difference to you? To someone who has that condition?

Social Questions for Students

- When giving advice to someone in your peer group, for what kinds of problems would you use "I" and for what would you use "you"?
- Do you take constructive criticism or suggestions well? What would your friends say?

Lesson 8I—Aligning Words and Actions

Key Concepts
aligning actions and words, **implication**
Special Materials/Media
none, except space for movement
Intro Questions/Thoughts for Students

- We think of communication as mainly with words, but how much meaning do we simultaneously convey with our physical actions? Aside from nodding "yes" or shaking our head "no," how often do we rely on physical gestures to communicate, and how do we interpret that?

Activity

In groups of three, students come to the front of the room. One of the three steps outside the class (this will be student 3). Student 1 then reads a slip of paper silently with a message, such as "Do your math homework" or "Would you like to come to my party?" Student 1 gets one minute to silently act out the message to Student 2. Student 2 is not to say what they think the message is, just receive it. Student 3 then is brought in and student 2 must again act out the message to student 3, but this time it is done as charades where student 3 may guess out loud and student 2 may confirm responses or guide them. After student 3 guesses the perceived message (or a time limit is reached), student 3's perceived message is compared with student 1's.

An alternate version is to pick an object. Student 1 may only describe it to student 2 (but cannot use physical movement or name it). Student 2 must then only act out the object or its use without words (or looking at it if the object is in the room) to student 3.

Follow-up Questions/Discussions

- Were the messages conveyed to student 3 more often correct or incorrect? What were the hardest things to communicate: verbs, nouns, or places? Why do you think that is?
- Besides shaking or nodding our head, what are ways we add meaning to the words we use? Can a body movement (or tone) change the meaning? Try saying "Yeah, right" with different meaning based on tone and actions.
- If meaning can be distorted by changing actions into words, what about words into other words? Go to Google translate and type in a famous phrase ("To be or not to be, that is the question" or "The only thing we have to fear is fear itself"). Translate the phrase into another language,

translate that translation into a third (preferably non-Western) language,[7] and then translate it back into English. What did you get?

Social Questions for Students

- When you have disagreements, are they over differences of opinion or differences in understanding, such as when your parents say to do something but don't specifically say "now"? How can you tell the difference and avoid misinterpretation?
- Have you ever had in mind what you want to say but couldn't find the words in the moment? What did you do?

Lesson 8J—Indirection

Key Concepts
effective communication by effective (direct or indirect) phrasing
Special Materials/Media
Access to newspaper or Internet advice columns
Intro Questions/Thoughts for Students

- When someone asks you for advice, is it better to be direct and blunt or to "soft sell" by being more indirect and reassuring? If it depends on who is asking and what they are asking about, try to make up general rules (If it is a ________ asking about a ______ kind of problem, be direct/indirect).

Activity

Students should look for advice columns and study how the responses are phrased; when is the advice direct, and when is it indirect or reassuring? Does the advice-giver start with advice or first an acknowledgment of the problem? What else does the advice-giver say?

Students can then write out "typical problems" students their age might encounter:

- put off homework and now can't get it done;
- not invited to a party;
- thinks someone likes them but is not sure;
- doesn't know how to tell parents they don't like or want to do a family activity.

Students then take turns formulating a response in an advice column way.

Follow-up Questions/Discussions

- If the person asking the question already knows about the problem, why does the advice-giver acknowledge or restate the problem? Does that help the asker to know they have been heard? Also, does it help the advice-seeker to know how the advice-giver sees the problem? How does that help?
- Can advice be both blunt and direct but still be reassuring?

Social Questions for Students

- Do you ever ask for advice just to talk about a problem rather than to get advice? Does it feel good to just talk about problems without necessarily seeking an immediate solution to them?
- Think of a problem you have, then write it out as if you were asking an online advisor for help. Wait a day, then write a response as if you were the online advisor responding to the letter you wrote.

Lesson 8K—Feeling in the Pink, or Are You Blue?

Key Concepts
color as visual persuasion, **implied messaging**
Special Materials/Media
Access to Internet or magazines
Intro Questions/Thoughts for Students

- Do colors mean something or imply certain ideas? What does the color red imply to you by itself? In context, when does it mean something good, and when does it mean something bad? Green? Blue? White? Black? Is there an implied "language of color"?
- Does the meaning of color change by culture? What color is associated with marriage in the United States, and what color in China? How did we get to have two colors mean the same thing? Is there logic to what colors mean?

Activity

In groups, have students brainstorm associations of the color spectrum (red, orange, yellow, green, blue, indigo, and violet), as well as white, black, and clear (no color), with meanings or imagery. Students should try to think of positive and negative associations or circumstances for each color if they can. Students should then share and make a compiled list.

Students can follow up in two ways. First, make a list of words on a slide presentation or pieces of paper but put some in the "wrong color" (put "grass" in blue and "sky" in green, or "heaven" in red and "hell" in blue) along with other words that are in the "right" colors as determined by the class ("fast" in red). Showing these words to non-classmates (such as friends or parents), do the subjects notice anything (or anything "wrong") about the words?

Alternatively, students can think of types of products (cleaning products, health products, cars, money services, etc.) and think what colors, in their opinion, "should" be associated with that kind of product. Students should then test their hypothesis by observing ads.[8]

Follow-up Questions/Discussions

- If "grass" means the same in any color, how can the color be "wrong"? Is there a second message (such as quality) that is conveyed by color?
- Are colors used not only to convey a message but to affect you or to put you in a mood? Can it be like the tone and inflection in saying, "Thank you"? Have the class look up paint companies (such as Glidden or Sherwin-Williams) that describe colors as reflecting certain moods to see if they correlate.
- Is there a difference between the color being "wrong" and "not right"?
- When you pre-guessed colors with a product and then looked for them, did you notice them because you were right or because you were now looking for that color to confirm you were right (**confirmation bias**)?

Social Questions for Students

- What is your favorite color? Is there something it represents to you? Have students group themselves by favorite color. Does the color mean the same to everyone in a group?
- When you expect something to happen one way (or a person to act a certain way) and another thing happens, how do you know when it is "wrong" (and perhaps needs correction) and when it is just different (and you need to adjust)?
- For you, what are the "colors" of abstract ideas such as friendship, love, or hate? Why?

Lesson 8L—Text vs. Context

Key Concepts

background as supplying meaning to messaging (**context**)

Special Materials/Media

camera, settings, costumes

Intro Questions/Thoughts for Students

- When is it OK to steal, say $25? If your family were starving or you needed cash for medicine and had no other way? How about to buy a cool shirt? Looking at the background or surrounding circumstances is called looking *in context*.
- How much do you judge things in context? Do you ever try to not look at context? When is that helpful, and when is that not?

Activity

Students use a candy bar, snack, or drink and take multiple camera shots of a person consuming it. It has to be the same person holding and consuming the product the same way, but the background is changed. Make one setting a sports scene, another a fun party, another a library or office, or any other place you wish. The pictures are shown to people outside who are asked to provide adjectives that they think describe the food *based on the person's face* (which is the same in all pics).

Alternatively, you can show pictures of the same person texting but with different background scenes (library, lunch, in front of a car wreck, etc.), asking viewers to speculate what the person is texting, again, *just based on the texter's facial expression*.

Have the class compare responses to backgrounds for a pattern.

Follow-up Questions/Discussions

- Were there differences? Did the differences reflect the background setting? Were there any descriptions specific to the background, such as "it gives you energy" for the sports scene or "it's elegant and classy" with a formal background?
- Do you think people who were affected by the background were intentionally ignoring the instructions or unintentionally? Do we all take in background without thinking about it?
- Do you think ad-makers think carefully about the background to the product in order to better sell it? Look at some ads and see.
- If context does affect how we evaluate things, do we do this with people as well as objects? Do the results of the texting experiment reflect this?

Social Questions for Students

- How do we come to make assumptions about people and things we don't fully know yet? If you saw a picture of an apple in a bowl of fresh fruit, would you assess the apple's quality differently than if you saw that same apple in a garbage can? As a bonus, spend a day taking pictures of just the *context* of your life, the background pics to all your chosen (versus compulsory) activities but without you in the pic. What might people who don't know you assume about you based simply on your context?

Lesson 8M—Stranger in a Strange Land

Key Concepts

assumptions and presumptions from unfamiliar context

Special Materials/Media

Access to foreign print ads

Intro Questions/Thoughts for Students

- When you find yourself in a strange place or situation, how do you figure out what is going on? Do you start with picking out common or recognizable things, or do you take in the entire situation at once? Do you start with a presumption that things or people are similar to the way you are used to or different?

Activity

Students should look for an ad that depicts people (preferably single shot or print ad for simplicity) and is printed in a language foreign to the student. For the ad, they should write out:

- What is the "story" behind the ad (such as the situation or problem that the product addresses)?
- What are the relationships of the people depicted? Who are friends? Who is related?
- How is the situation resolved? What happens after the scene?

For each question, students should indicate their basis for their answers. What clues are they considering, and, even more, what presumptions are they making about how the culture depicted operates?

Follow-up Questions/Discussions

- Based on the ads and how you interpreted them, are there "universal rules" of culture, such as the way families interact or what smiling or shaking hands means?
- Were there any parts that you had trouble interpreting? What questions might you want to ask of the people in the ad to get a better idea?

- Were any of your deductions based on things you heard about that culture (indirect source)? What might be the advantages and disadvantages of making deductions based on secondhand knowledge?

Social Questions for Students

- We often assume people think like us and have the same motivations and values as we do, but how can you make sure that is correct with your classmates? When is it OK to assume people think alike and when is it better not to do so?
- Are there any assumptions made about you that you wish people wouldn't make? Perhaps the entire class can write these down on anonymous slips of paper ("I wish people wouldn't assume I am/do ___________") for the teacher to read out in front of the class.

Lesson 8N—Can You See the Real Me, Can Ya?

Key Concepts
stereotype depictions, persuasion and stereotypes disguised as research
Special Materials/Media
Access to Google or another online search engine
Intro Questions/Thoughts for Students

- When we don't know something, we ask someone, hopefully someone without bias. When you do a search on the Internet, whom are you asking?
- Search engines like Google use algorithms, or complex sets of rules, to decide what you most likely want when you search for something on the Internet. What are the advantages and disadvantages of letting a computer select your search results?

Activity

Students are to conduct two sets of searches on the Internet. First, they should image-search "People in __________" or "Typical ____________" filling in the blank with their own city, state, or region. Assuming they know nothing about their own region, what would they conclude about "typical" people in their region based on the first image? Is it accurate? What is missing? How many images (assume they are numbered from left to right) before there is an image the student feels adequately represents them or their typical life?

As a second search, students should all-search (text) "Why do __________" filling in the name for people of their locale ("Bostonians," "Texans,") and let autocomplete finish the suggested search sentence. Students should write down the top three to five suggestions of autocomplete and then write a response as if someone they did not know asked them the question. The student should indicate in her response whether she believes what is suggested as a "typical" activity or belief is, in fact, typical or just a stereotype.

Follow-up Questions/Discussions

- Were the images more of daily life or of exceptional or special events and people? Why do you think that is (remember, the images are picked based on previous searches)?
- If people who don't know you were to assume they did based on the images, what extra information would you want them to know to be accurate?
- What was the average picture number for which your class members found an image they felt accurately represented them? What was the range? Why do you think that was? How do people who found themselves depicted early feel as compared to people who only found themselves depicted much later?
- Were any of the auto-suggested questions funny or offensive? Why do you think people ask such things? Did you find some **stereotyping** (overgeneralizing) of your life or your community?
- Since you know your community, you know which images and ideas are stereotypes and are incorrect, but what about if you searched for other communities that you did not know a lot about? Might you believe overgeneralized depictions of them?
- Should we just accept search results? Is it enough to say, "The computer says . . . "? What should we be thinking about as we view search results? What can we do to guard against stereotypes and untruthful depictions about others?

Social Questions for Students

- Has anyone been upset with you because you don't look or act "the way you should"? When should you consider how those around you act or look? When should you not?
- Have you ever been caught in a **feedback loop**? This is where you are told or shown how others think you should be, and then you assume you should follow suit, thus confirming the beliefs of the person who told you in the first place. This is often how fashion trends or fads ("everyone's doing it") take off. When is this a bad thing, and when is it OK?

Lesson 8O—Alphabetically, *After* Comes Before *Before* . . . Weird, Huh?

Key Concepts

persuasion through **juxtaposition**

Special Materials/Media

Access to ads

Intro Questions/Thoughts for Students

- The teacher should put two unrelated pictures of people next to each other and ask the students, "What do you think?" or to reflect on the pictures without any other prompt. Have students write their reflection. Have students read their reflections aloud, noting how often students compared and contrasted the two pictures without any instruction to do so, simply because the pictures were side by side (or **juxtaposed**). Ask students why they think they did that.

Activity

Students should find an ad that has "before" and "after" pictures. They are then to write out a story of what is depicted and what happened in between the pictures. Students should make specific references to objects or things in the picture as support for their deductions.

For two fun follow-ups, the teacher may announce a random strange event (volcano erupts, aliens land) that must be included in the story as happening between the two pictures. Students may also be asked to act out a "living diorama," in which the teacher calls out an event, such as "studies for test" or "plays in big game," to which the students must present two freeze-frame depictions of what happened before and after the event.

Follow-up Questions/Discussions

- Messengers such as advertisers can convey things without directly saying them (such as what happens between the pictures). This is called *implying* something.[9] What are the advantages and disadvantages of implying a message rather than just saying it?
- How we interpret implied messages is also based on assumptions we make. If you see a "before" picture of two people holding glasses of water, and in the "after" picture one of them is cleaning up broken glass, do most of us assume he dropped it? Why? When is that OK to do and when might that cause problems?

Social Questions for Students

- What do people assume about you that you wish they did not?
- If you made a "before/after" pic of this school year (before being just before school started, after being today), what would it look like? What might people assume from the picture that might be true or might not?

Lesson 8P—Drawn In

Key Concepts

visceral vs. rational consideration of messages, **pathos** vs. **logos** in persuasion

Special Materials/Media

Access to ads

Intro Questions/Thoughts for Students

- What kinds of decisions do you make with a removed, analytical (**rational**) approach to deciding and in which do you use a more emotional, gut (**visceral**) response? Which is best for deciding where to go to eat? How to invest money? What to buy a friend for a birthday present?
- In choosing whether to use more intellect or emotion to decide something, how much do people try to persuade you to use one or the other? What clues tell you what the messenger is appealing to, your intellect or emotion?

Activity

Students should bring in ads and decide if the appeal (persuasive technique) is more to one's rational (removed) side or to one's emotional (drawn in) side. Some clues that might help:

- Does the ad use numbers or graphs?
- Does the ad make you a removed observer (faraway shot or putting the depicted scene in a frame so as to make clear you are outside) or does the ad try to draw you in (close-up shots or someone in the ad is looking right at you) inviting you into the scene?
- Does the ad depict "emotional tugs" such as a cute animal or depict a common fear?
- Does the ad purport to offer a "common sense" or logical solution?

Follow-up Questions/Discussions

- Are some kinds of products more geared to emotion ("Join the fun!") and some more to logic ("It works")? Why is that?
- The use of emotion to persuade (**pathos**) and the use of facts, logic, or reasoning (**logos**) are considered separate techniques, but did you ever find them combined? How so?[10]
- Did you find any "false logos," where the ad seemed like it was using numbers or logic, but it was deceptive, such as saying "thousands have tried it" or "only one proven to work," but then you read it was the only one tested?
- Movie posters often have the main actors looking right at the viewer; why do you think that is?
- If all messaging uses pathos or logos, where do you see it in political ads, at school, or at home?

Social Questions for Students

- Is it OK to use someone's fear of something to persuade them? How about the fear of having no friends if they don't spend a lot of money to look good? How about the fear of harm if they use drugs? Do you ever use fear to get your way?

Lesson 8Q—Oh, What a Knight!

Key Concepts

effect of auditory cues on perception

Special Materials/Media

Picture of a knight, three to four theme songs (can be obtained from the Internet)

Intro Questions/Thoughts for Students

- Stop the class and be silent for a minute. What did you hear? Whatever you are hearing, do you hear that when it is not silent? The answer is most probably yes (the sound waves are still vibrating against your ear drum), but you don't notice it. Does it still impact you?
- How much does sound affect how we perceive things? How does music (such as a villain's theme song that plays whenever he enters[11]) affect what we think about him or what we anticipate will happen?

Activity

Divide the students into four groups. Tell each they will write a story based on a picture and accompanying music. Each group should work away from the others and not hear or look at the other groups' materials. Each group is then given (secretly) the *same* picture of a knight or castle.

Each group is given a link, however, to four different kinds of background music:

- ominous, scary music
- heroic, adventure music
- fun, light-hearted music
- romantic music

When the groups are ready, have them take turns playing the music and reading the story. After all have gone, show that they had the same picture.

Follow-up Questions/Discussions

- Were there differences in how each group saw the picture? Was it hard to adjust to another group's way of seeing the knight?
- Where else is sound used to affect how you see things? In stores, what kind of music do they play (and what mood do they want you to be in)? How about TV shows? Do they use music to affect your mood and how you see things? Compare the opening themes of a comedy, a mystery, and an action show.
- Why do TV shows use canned (inserted) laughter? Why does it help make the audience laugh?
- Can other senses such as smell, taste, or touch affect how we perceive things?

Social Questions for Students

- Do you have your "go to" music for certain moods? When you are sad, do you prefer sad music that aligns with your mood or happy music to help you not be so sad? What is your "get excited" music?
- If you were a movie character with a set background theme every time you entered a scene, what song or kind of music would it be?

Lesson 8R—Noisy Theater of the Mind

Key Concepts

sound as influencing imagery

Special Materials/Media

Miscellaneous objects to make sound effects

Intro Questions/Thoughts for Students

- Have you ever had an image in your mind of the way something looks but then been disappointed or thrown off when you saw how it really looked (or how someone else portrayed it)?
- Is it easier to use imagination with just hearing something or just seeing something? Why?

Activity

A Foley artist is a person who adds everyday sounds to movies, like using crispy cereal to sound like walking on gravel or imitating with their mouth a creaky door opening. Students should be divided into groups with each group preparing to tell other students a fairy tale. The groups should have a narrator, various students taking different voice parts, and some in the group being Foley artists who add sound effects. As an added challenge, the group must stop at some point and do a fifteen- to thirty-second ad for a product related to the story (Pete's porridge, Little Red's riding hoods), complete with slogan and jingle. The groups take turns presenting with the listeners sitting or lying comfortably but with their eyes closed.

Follow-up Questions/Discussions

- Was it hard to come up with ways to imitate sounds? Was it fun? Why?
- Was it hard to not talk or to not make noise when it was your turn to be quiet? Why so?
- For listening, how did the sounds affect your picturing the story?

Social Questions for Students

- We are often so busy seeing that we miss a lot of interesting sounds. When we focus less on seeing, we appreciate the sounds more, even if for a little while. The same is true for all the activities we do. If we are so busy trying to get the next thing done (or worrying how we will do it), can we miss the fun and good times in the moment? What is a good thing you have in the background of your daily life that you rarely take time to appreciate, like having meals when you want them? What do your parents wish they had appreciated more when they were younger?

- Try walking to class for a day without making noise and just listening. For each walk, what is something new you heard or something you never noticed before?

NOTES

1. See also discussion at lesson 5I.
2. See chapter 3.
3. In archaeology, for example, there has been a reexamination as to whether ancient Egyptians were as "death obsessed" as has traditionally been thought. Were they so focused on the afterlife, or do we think that because we keep digging up their longer-lasting graveyards rather than their built-over living centers?
4. See also lesson 5B.
5. See chapter 5.
6. See lesson 8B.
7. Don't just keep changing the destination language of the original English. You need to put the translated words (such as those just into Spanish) now over to the left-side "translate from" box (or hit the reverse arrows) and then pick a third language (such as Thai or Chinese) for the other box, then repeat by translating the third language phrase back into English.
8. This can also be done for different demographic groups, like boys, girls, young, old, professionals, etc.
9. See also lesson 8I.
10. The third type of persuasion, **ethos** (appeal by the spokesperson), is addressed in lesson 3D.
11. Google or use YouTube to find Darth Vader's theme as an example.

Chapter Nine

Telling the Truth

Media literacy and its cousin consumer economics seem to be recent arrivals in the deconstruction and analysis of communication, but in fact they have been a part of mankind's decoding tools for a very long time. Schools that say, "We need to teach media literacy" are overlooking that every time a language or literature teacher challenges students to find meaning in a passage, they are engaging in a media literacy exercise. Every art teacher who challenges his or her students to find or express meaning through nonverbal techniques is part of a media literacy chain that stretches back perhaps forty thousand years to early man creating and viewing cave paintings.

James Madison, the father of our Constitution, wrote more than 230 years ago as to our societal need as a nation for diversity of opinion. In Federalist Paper #10, he insisted that a necessary check on tyranny and oppression was nothing less than a diverse body of people and their varying opinions. In such a mix, for any idea or point of view to gain the support of a majority of the people, it had to be acceptable to a variety of those different perspectives.

Today, we have achieved a diverse population beyond any Madison could have dreamed of. What we need to do now is learn how to listen to each other, take in all of the varied ways we communicate this diversity of thought, and figure out how to separate and hold on to the good ideas held in common, for the common good.

Much is being said of late about "fake news" amid worry for how quickly misinformation spreads across social networks. An old adage, at least one hundred years old (and ascribed in various forms to everyone from Jonathan Swift to Mark Twain), is that *a lie can travel halfway around the world while truth is still putting on its shoes*. In today's world of instant media, truth sometimes hasn't even woken up.

Bending the truth. Not giving the full story. Shading. Dissimulating. Falsifying. The prevalence of so many synonyms and euphemisms for lying can make one despair at what humans have done with one of the greatest gifts we have: language and the art of communication. Whether being exhorted to consume tangible goods or intangible ideas, people today are bombarded with prepackaged solutions that promise a better life, but is that better life for the consumer or the purveyor of what's being sold?

Like any tool, the ability to communicate can be used for good or ill will, and so we must teach people, especially our youth, how to recognize improper use and how to defend themselves against harm. [1]

See **Lesson 9A—To Tell the Truth**

CHAPTER 9 ACCOMPANYING LESSONS

Lesson 9A—To Tell the Truth

Key Concepts

detecting who is telling the truth versus who is lying, **tells**

Special Materials/Media

None

Intro Questions/Thoughts for Students

- How can you tell when someone is telling the truth or not? What clues can you discover in how a person recounts a story to judge whether or not you should believe it? What physical signs might you look for?

Activity

This is a variation of the old TV game show *To Tell the Truth.* Three students are taken out into the hall and are asked for some interesting trivia about themselves (such as one met a celebrity at an airport, one won a tournament, or one has an unusual secret hobby). The teacher then brings the three students in before the class and announces that one of the students has an interesting fact and describes it generally ("They met a famous person while on vacation"). The rest of the class then asks questions of the three about the topic (it's best to mandate a rotational response, so question 1 goes to panelist 1, question 2 to panelist 2, question 3 to 3, then back to 1 so all are asked). The panelists must observe these rules:

- The one for whom the story is true may not lie and must always answer truthfully.

- The other two are free to make up stuff, but it must be believable (their job is to try to convince people).

At the end of the questioning (either timed or two to three questions for each questioner), the class votes on which panelist they believe the story is about. The truth teller is then revealed.

Alternatively, this can be done with three teachers as panelists.

Follow-up Questions/Discussions

- How did you choose your questions? Were they more open-ended or yes/no?
- Did the questioners each ask their own questions or did they build off each other (follow-up)? Which is more effective?
- Did anyone ask, "Are you telling the truth?" or "Are you lying?" Was that helpful?
- Aside from answers to questions, what other things did you notice, such as body movement or hesitating in answering, especially for the ones making up the story? These are called **tells** and are used by many people, from police to poker players, to assess believability.
- Are some people better at faking it than others? Why do you think that is?

Social Questions for Students

- How do we draw the line between exaggerating a story to make it more interesting and outright lying?
- Is lying ever OK? Is there a difference between lying about meeting a famous person and lying about copying someone's homework?
- How can we detect "tells" in messaging in the real world?

NOTE

1. Giving youth the tools to decide for themselves what products and ideas should be a part of their life harkens back to a slogan of the 1960s counterculture, a phrase that, if said by a young consumer, may be the best sign of a successful media literacy education: "Not with my life, you don't!"

Glossary

Note: Where possible, we have steered away from technical economic definitions to assist the teacher unfamiliar with economics to have an understanding that he can then pass on to his students. Lessons that directly address the term appear in parentheses.

Accessory An additional product that **complements** an already existing one by making the original product more useful, versatile, or attractive. (2F)

Ad hominem fallacy A technique in which one tries to refute an argument by attacking the proponent of the argument by some attribute such as their motive, bias, or credentials.

Affectation, affected An artificial way of communicating designed to impress in order to gain **panache**. Also called **posing**. (4D)

Anecdotal evidence Fallacious proof by which a general premise is supported by isolated examples rather than general data.

Aspirational buying, aspirational thinking In terms of demographics, when consumers (usually younger ones) imitate, as best that they can, the consumption habits of older consumers in an attempt to gain age **panache**. (6F, 7M)

Bandwagon effect A type of **ethos appeal**, it is the psychological nudge to do (or consume) something because others are doing it, also known as FOMO (Fear of Missing Out). (4C)

Barter system A nonmonetary system of exchange in which goods and services are exchanged for other goods and services. (2C)

Behavioral economics A branch of economic study that includes, if not focuses on, psychological factors on human decision making.

Brand impression An occasion where a potential consumer sees or interacts with a product or its brand, the idea being that the cumulative effect of each encounter leads to a familiarity and thus positive feelings toward the product, leading in turn to a desire to consume it. (3B, 3L)

Bundling The practice of offering multiple, usually related, goods and services together in one sale at a lower price than if each item were purchased separately.

Centrics Common, core needs or desires of a particular demographic group that can be appealed to in order to nudge a potential consumer to desire a good or service.

Classification A psychological desire, often seen in tweens, to put valuation on similar items relative to each other.

Command economy An economic system characterized by the economic decision making being done by the government or its agents, as opposed to individual buyers and sellers.

Complements, complementary goods Goods that are so linked to another good (such as peanut butter and jelly) that demand for the two track each other, or an increase in the price of one will make demand for the other decrease. (2F)

Conditioning Training a subject to give a standard, predictable response to repeated stimuli through training and reinforcement.

Confirmation bias The tendency to interpret data as being aligned with or supporting the interpreter's already established conclusions or beliefs. (8B)

Conspicuous consumption Overtly consuming a good or service so that one may gain **panache** from others seeing the consumption as a status privilege. (4B, 4D)

Consumer economics Heavily overlapping with **behavioral economics**, it is the study of the psychological factors that influence a person's decision to obtain, buy, or consume something.

Consumer sovereignty The theory that a producer/consumer (seller/buyer) market is driven more by the desires and demands of the consumers, with producers responding to those desires. (5I)

Coolhunting Seeking of new or rising trends (often by observing people perceived as trend-setters) in order to gain a marketing advantage.

Cost-benefit analysis The primary method of decision making in economics, whereby a person weighs (consciously or subconsciously) both the advantages and disadvantages of one option against another.

Curate, curated Selectively choosing and presenting a subset of items from a larger group based on a particular theme or to project an idea or impression.

Currency A form of money generally recognized as acceptable payment within a community. (2C)

Diminishing return, law of The situation or tendency wherein a consumer receives less benefit or enjoyment (**utility**) out of a good or service acquired despite investing (putting in) the same amount of resources or cost to acquire that good or service previously. In more casual terms, it's not getting the same bang for the buck one used to. (2E)

Dog whistle An indirect or implied message meant to communicate with a particular group, usually placed within a more general message. (5H)

Drivers (of tween decision making) As proposed by David Siegel et al., they are the deeper, subconscious psychological needs that coalesce into **centrics**. (7B)

Economic good A product or service that is desired and seen as having value by consumers.

Editorial An article written more with an intent to give the writer's opinion or views on a topic than to present objective news or information on it. (8F)

Entrepreneurship The knowledge, training, or special skills a producer brings to the creation of a good. Sometimes considered a fourth factor of **production**.

Ethos appeal A method of trying to persuade people to accept **information** or messaging because of the authority, credibility, or appeal of the speaker. Also called an endorsement. (3D)

External Honorific Booty A good or service whose utility comes from **conspicuous consumption**, or other people seeing and admiring the consumption as a privilege of status. (4B)

Extraneous variable In conducting experiments, something that you are not looking for or even mindful of that affects the experiment's data or results. (7O)

Eye candy Superficially attractive or entertaining visual images. (3I)

Factors of production The resources that go into making or producing a good, usually subdivided into land (raw materials), labor (work force), and capital (tools, machines, and money). Sometimes **entrepreneurship** is added as a fourth factor.

Fads Intense, temporary interest or popularity in a product or activity, leading to a rush in consumption due to the **bandwagon effect**. (4C)

Fallacy An argument based on unsound reasoning or improper factors.

False scarcity Creating an impression that a good or service is limited, by either artificially limiting the good's availability (such as to time or amount) or using equivocation to give that impression. (2B)

Feedback loop A phenomenon whereby media, reporting a purported trend, inspire consumers to follow the trend (due to the **bandwagon effect**), which then seemingly confirms the initial report. Often a starting point for **fads**. (8B)

Flattery A marketing technique whereby the potential consumer is complimented as part of the sales pitch, inducing the consumer to feel good in relation to the product and therefore buy it. (7E)

Focus nudge A **nudge** for the receiver to concentrate on a particular point or follow a particular line of thought.

Free good A good or resource that is abundant and there is seemingly no cost to utilizing it.

Free-market (capitalist) economy An economic system characterized by the economic decision making being done by individual buyers and sellers. (5A)

GRAIL An acronym for five major demographic attributes of consumers: Gender, Race, Age, Income, and Lifestyle. (5A)

Hasty generalization fallacy A **fallacy** whereby a conclusion is drawn from insufficient evidence, often utilized to ascribe a characteristic of a few or some members of a group to all its members (from an insufficient **sample size**). (8G)

Hedging Subtly limiting or equivocating a claim so as to reduce the guarantee or assertion made in the claim. (3G)

Honorific Booty Goods or services acquired more for the psychological **utility** (good feeling) of possessing it rather than practical **utility**.

Hyperbole Exaggerated claims or statements that a reasonable person would see as a tool of promotion but not a statement of fact.

Implied messaging, implication Suggesting a statement through indirect words or actions without directly stating the message. (8I, 8K)

Inflation The condition wherein the price of goods rises because there is greater demand (and therefore money offered) than there are available goods. (2C)

Influencers Members of a community who, through their social standing or power, can **nudge** others toward actions and beliefs. (7J)

Information Facts or data presented without motive or bias, as opposed to **persuasion**. (1B)

Internal Honorific Booty A good or service whose **utility** comes from the good feeling the consumer has from possessing/utilizing it, regardless of whether others know, such as a keepsake. (4A)

Investment (money or time) An outlay (payment) of goods or services today in anticipation of a delayed but greater return (payment) in the future. (6F)

Juxtaposition Placing items, whether physical objects, pictures, or statements, side by side to invite comparison and contrast of them. (8O)

KGOY (Kids Getting Older Younger) The phenomenon that children today are more exposed to and are more aware of facets of society, including **marketing** and consumption, than previous generations, often to a negative psychological effect. (7M)

Logo A picture or graphic design used by a company to instantly bring that company to a viewer's mind. (3L)

Logos appeal A method of trying to persuade people to accept **information** or messaging because of logic or rational factors such as data. (8P)

Marginal utility The benefit (such as satisfaction) a consumer gets from consuming or utilizing one additional unit of a good or service, such as the amount of thirst quenched by drinking an additional soda. (2E)

Market, marketing, marketer Presenting **information** or other demonstration in order to **persuade** the receiver into consuming (usually in exchange for money) a product or service.

Market penetration The amount (such as percentage of population) a product is consumed within a particular **niche** or demographic group. (6B)

Media literacy The ability to critically evaluate, understand, and decode messages to discern the difference between **information** and **persuasion**, to see what is both explicitly and implicitly messaged, for the consumer of information ultimately to have more control of the diet of messaging they consume.

Medium of exchange Something, such as money, that acts as a middle or common reference point (such as value) in purchasing goods and services. (2C)

Monetary vs. sentimental value Whether a good is deemed to have **utility** based on how much other consumers would pay for it or the subjective (psychological) value deemed by the consumer. (4A)

Negative Honorific Booty A good or service whose **utility** comes from society's perceiving such consumption as a negative act, lending to the consumer's **panache** for being independent or a rebel.

Neoclassical economics A traditional economic approach that focuses as much as possible only on mathematical description of the rational factors that influence economic decisions, especially as to producers and consumers.

Niche That part of the general population of potential buyers (GRAIL) wherein a product will sell well, and thus the consumers to whom a seller should pitch his or her goods. Also called segments. (5A)

Niche targeting A marketer focusing their sales appeal to a particular **niche**, often in a way unappealing to other niches. (5A)

Nonrational factors in decision making Factors (often emotional or visceral) beyond traditional factors such as price, quality, and availability that may be weighed in economic decision making.

Norm A behavior or belief that is seen as the standard, accepted, and proper one of a society, with behaviors or beliefs contrary to the norm being unusual, socially deviant, or even possibly morally wrong. (6H)

Nudge/nudging As conceived by Richard Thaler, any factor that alters people's behavior in a predictable way without forbidding any options or significantly changing their economic incentives.

Panache Having a style or manner, usually indicating superior socioeconomic status, that stands out and is admired by others.

Passive cool When a consumer acquires **panache** by assuming a public demeanor of not caring what others think, ironically earning the admiration of others. (4E)

Pathos appeal A method of trying to persuade people to accept **information** or messaging because of emotion (such as sympathy). (8P)

Pecuniary emulation When consumers imitate, as best that they can, the consumption habits of those in higher socioeconomic statuses in an attempt to gain **panache**.

Persona A personality or character shown to others. (3C)

Persuasion, persuade The act of presenting **information** with intent to affect the receiver's opinion, belief, or point of view. (1B)

Posing, poser Acting in an affected manner, usually to impress others. (7B)

Preconception A view or opinion of something one has before actually encountering it. Can lead to **confirmation bias**. (8G)

Price effect The impact that a change in price has on consumer demand for a product.

Rare goods (rarity) Goods that there are few of, regardless of demand.

Sample size In **social sciences**, it is the number (and makeup) of the group of people tested from which the experimenter draws general conclusions about larger population groups. As such, the sample size needs to be representative of the larger group. (5B)

Sampling error When a tester draws incorrect or improper conclusions because the **sample size** did not accurately reflect the larger group. (5F)

Scarce goods (scarcity) Goods that there are fewer of than demand for it; i.e., more people want it than there are units of it available. (2A, 2C)

Scientific method A method of procedure that allows for systematic (and repeatable) observations so that conclusions may be objectively drawn.

Self-branding When a consumer identifies themselves as loyal to a particular brand, based on either rational or nonrational factors, which then **nudges** the consumer to choose that brand over others. (3C)

Seriation A psychological desire, often seen in tweens, to put groups of items in a logical sequence or order.

Slant A way of conveying information favorable to one particular view or interpretation of the **information**, rather than in an objective, neutral manner. (8D)

Social construct An idea or understanding that organically grows out of societal views and becomes accepted as truth.

Social science The scientific study of humans and human relationships (as opposed to physical sciences that study physical phenomena), using **scientific methods** to observe, quantify, and draw conclusions. (1A)

Stacking Skewing experiments, data, or their presentation in a way that helps **market** a good or service.

Stalagmite effect A phenomenon whereby incremental changes accumulate to form a significant effect over time, as stalagmites are created from drops of calcite over many years. (5D)

Stereotype A generalization made about a larger population based upon a few members, often the result of a **sampling error**. (8B)

Substitutes A good that may be purchased as a replacement or fill in for another, such as turkey for chicken at a deli. Usually, a price increase of one increases demand for the other. (2F)

Tacit pressure The **nudge** that societal or situational norms place upon individuals, usually members of minority populations, indirectly messaged to conform to the expectations of the majority population. (6D, 7L)

Teaching format—Circle talk A classroom style generally composed of students exchanging ideas through discussion. Generally more open and free-form, allowing students more time and space to discuss.

Teaching format—Fishbowl A classroom technique generally composed of a fast-paced, rotating participatory style designed to promote a more quickly evolving discussion than a **circle talk** format.

Teaching format—Improv format A classroom technique generally composed of giving students a prompt or setup that they must act out, incorporating extraneous elements or information after a short (or no) preparation time.

Teaching format—Socratic seminar A teaching technique wherein students focus on discussing guided questions. More formal that **circle talk** but more open than a **fishbowl** format.

Tells Inadvertent behavior or mannerism that reveals the person's intent, meaning, or even honesty. (9A)

Traditional economy An economic system characterized by the economic decision making being done mindful of community customs or beliefs, such as traditional clothing (cowboy boots in Texas) or social/religious restrictions.

Utility The benefit a consumer gets from having and using a good, whether tangible (food as nutrition), personal (the comfort feeling of a particular food), or esoteric (the admiration of others from eating certain foods). (2K, 4C)

Viewer substitute A person in an ad that acts as the stand-in for the viewer of the ad; the person whom the ad viewer is meant to empathize with. (7E)

Viral advertising A marketing technique whereby marketers use consumers (or apparent consumers) to market products, often through social networks. (3A)

Visceral processing Responding to information based on inward ("gut") feelings rather than logic or reasoning. (8P)

Bibliography

Advertising and Promoting to Kids (APK). 2002 convention program (sponsored by Kidscreen). 2002.

Crain, Caleb. "Why We Don't Read, Revisited." *The New Yorker*. June 14, 2018. https://www.newyorker.com/culture/cultural-comment/why-we-dont-read-revisited.

Freytag, Gustav. *Freytag's Technique of Drama: An Exposition of Dramatic Composition and Art*. London: Forgotten Books, 2015.

Henry, Holly K. M., and Dina L. G. Borzekowski. "The Nag Factor: How Do Children Convince Their Parents to Buy Unhealthy Foods?" Johns Hopkins University Bloomberg School of Public Health. August 11, 2011. https://www.jhsph.edu/news/news-releases/2011/borzekowski-nag-factor.html.

Krasniak, Michelle. "Visual Content and Social Media Marketing: New Research." Social Media Examiner. May 30, 2017. https://www.socialmediaexaminer.com/visual-content-and-social-media-marketing-new-research/.

Levitt, Steven D., and Stephen J. Dubner. *Freakonomics: A Rogue Economist Explores the Hidden Side of Everything*. New York: William Morrow, 2005.

Malabrigo, Victoria. "Visual Content on Social Media: 2017 Trends and Research." WNET/New York Public Media Interactive Engagement Group. March 13, 2017. https://ieg.wnet.org/2017/03/visual-content-social-media-2017-trends-research/.

McLeod, Saul. "Maslow's Hierarchy of Needs." Simply Psychology. https://www.simplypsychology.org/maslow.html.

McNeal, James U. *Kids as Customers: A Handbook of Marketing to Children*. New York: Lexington Books, 1992.

OpenClipart-Vectors. "Knight." Pixabay. https://pixabay.com/en/users/OpenClipart-Vectors-30363/.

"Randomizing Engine Site." Random.org. https://www.random.org/.

Ruskin, Gary. "Why They Whine: How Corporations Prey on Our Children." *Mothering Magazine*. July 1, 2003. http://www.mothering.com/10-0-0/html/10-3-0/10-3-whine97.shtml.

Siegel, David, Timothy Coffey, and Gregory Livingston. *The Great Tween Buying Machine: Marketing to Today's Tweens*. Ithaca, NY: Paramount Market Publishing, 2001.

Steiner, Peter. "On the Internet, Nobody Knows You're a Dog." *The New Yorker*. July 5, 1993.

Thaler, Richard, and Cass Sunstein. *Nudge: Improving Decisions about Health, Wealth and Happiness*. New York: Penguin Books, 2009.

Veblen, Thorstein. *The Theory of the Leisure Class*. New York: Macmillan, 1899.

Vom Wangenheim, Klaus Dieter. "Mountain." Pixabay. https://pixabay.com/en/switzerland-zermatt-mountains-snow-862870/.

Wasserman, Jim, and David Loveland. "More than Reality." *American School Board Journal* 204, no. 2 (April 2017).

Winkler, Joachim Marian. "Horse." Pixabay. https://pixabay.com/en/arabs-stallion-thoroughbred-arabian-1367173/.

About the Authors

Jim Wasserman has had two career lives: first as a business litigation attorney and then, for the past twenty-five years, as a humanities teacher specializing in media literacy, economics, government, history, and public speaking. Jim has been a pioneer in teaching and developing curricula regarding media literacy in secondary schools, starting as far back as the 1990s when he, ironically, was explaining social networking to teens! Jim has also been willing to throw himself into the media mix to better understand the Brave New World of media—from being an early adopter of social media and blogging to appearing on (and winning!) a national reality game show. Jim has published articles over the past thirty years on subjects ranging from law to religion to education, as well as editorials. He has recently retired and now lives in Granada, Spain, with his wife and two sons. Jim and his wife maintain a blog (yourthirdlife.com) on the financial, logistical, and lifestyle aspects of retirement, expatting, and travel.

David W. Loveland is a middle-school humanities teacher who has spent most of his career engaging his students in creative, cooperative, and critical activities such as Model Congress and Mock Trial to place them in the role of civic participant rather than simple observer. His professional goal is to use lessons from American history to give context and make sense of today's headlines. As media becomes more inundated with all kinds of dubious and contradictory information, Dave can most often be heard telling his students to check their research and go back to the source. He loves telling the stories of history and igniting a passion in his students to learn more about the world, the people in it, and themselves.

Dave and Jim, together, have published articles on education and media, which have been featured in education journals from America to Australia (and other countries beyond the letter "A").

www.ingramcontent.com/pod-product-compliance
Ingram Content Group UK Ltd.
Pitfield, Milton Keynes, MK11 3LW, UK
UKHW042036051026
476324UK00001BB/67

9 781475 842173